A Full
Net

Also from Islandport Press

Suddenly, the Cider Didn't Taste so Good
John Ford

Backtrack
V. Paul Reynolds

Bald Eagles, Bear Cubs, and Hermit Bill
Ron Joseph

Tributaries
Ryan Brod

Whatever It Takes
May Davidson

Tales From Misery Ridge
Paul Fournier

My Life in the Maine Woods
Annette Jackson

Nine Mile Bridge
Helen Hamlin

In Maine
John Cole

Ghost Buck
Dean Bennett

A Full Net

Fishing Stories from Maine and Beyond

Susan Daignault

ISLANDPORT PRESS

ISLANDPORT PRESS

Islandport Press
P.O. Box 10
Yarmouth, Maine 04096
www.islandportpress.com
info@islandportpress.com

First Edition: December 2023
Printed in the United States of America.
All photographs, unless otherwise noted, courtesy of Susan F. Daignault.

ISBN: 978-1-952143-64-9
Library of Congress Control Number: 2022948373

Dean L. Lunt | Editor-in-Chief, Publisher
Shannon M. Butler | Vice President
Emily A. Lunt | Book Designer

To Mom and Dad, with love beyond words.

Table of Contents

INTRODUCTION

I grew up in Blackstone, a small Massachusetts town on the Rhode Island border north of Providence. Mom and Dad were schoolteachers so they had summers off, which gave us the freedom to leave home the day school let out each spring and not return until a few days before classes started back up in the fall. We spent most of those summers camping on Cape Cod. I distinctly recall crying when leaving my beach buddies, but feeling elated when I returned to my hometown friends.

Our return to Blackstone life was packed with getting haircuts, restocking cupboards, and buying school supplies for the coming year. And we came back fully tanned, blond with sun-bleached hair, and strong from running, walking, and playing hard on the beach. We fished hard, too. Those summers spawned my love for the outdoors and fishing. We grew as a family together in love and support for one another. Then as we got older we went our separate ways, like many families, never forgetting our love for the sand in our toes, salt in our hair, and chasing the mighty striper.

During my junior year in high school, I began researching the service academies for my future college dreams. I was drawn to the United States Coast Guard Academy in New London, Connecticut due to its sea service and humanitarian missions of saving lives, environmental stewardship, and law enforcement. New London was also only a ninety-minute drive from home. In June 1979, still only seventeen years old, I showed up in New London for Swab Summer (the academy equivalent of boot camp). Four years later, on May 18, 1983, I was adorned with the slight shoulder boards of a newly christened ensign and shoved off for my first duty station, the Coast Guard cutter *Firebush*, in Kodiak, Alaska. All academy graduates had to go to sea for a two-year tour. I packed a fly rod that my classmates had gotten me, but did not have a clue how to fly fish. I had earned a Bachelor of Science in marine engineering; I had no clue how to use that, either. Little did I know that I'd stay on for thirty years, moving from Kodiak to Seattle to Lake Charles, Louisiana. After six years on active duty, I joined the reserves, transforming my full-time active-duty work to the part-time assignments I then did for twenty-four years, in addition to my civilian career as a safety professional.

Lake Charles proved scorching hot for this native New Englander, so it made sense to head north when I left active duty. Bath Iron Works was hiring safety engineers who inspected work at the shipyard, performed safety training, and enforced OSHA standards. They offered me a job over the phone and I accepted, so my partner, Karen Croteau, and I headed to Maine and a small coastal town only about three hours from where I grew up in Massachusetts. It was just beautiful.

Karen and I met in kindergarten. Her last name started with a *C*, mine with a *D*, so we were seated alphabetically next to one another. Sandy (my twin sister) is *Sa* and Susan is *Su* so Sandy was often right next to her, so I would switch seats with Sandy so I could sit closer to Karen. We became best friends in eighth grade, played three seasons of sports together and became

Karen and me at my Coast Guard retirement in 2013.

co-captains of most of our teams. We were also in the same college-track classes so we spent a lot of time together.

In Maine, we eventually moved to Harpswell and found the shoreline and a comfortable home right on the salt water, where I can gauge each fishing season by the water temperature and carefully map the striper migration to and from our backyard. While I await their annual arrival each May and mourn their departure in October, I fill the surrounding months with freshwater fishing, mostly using a fly rod, but at times I use spinning gear and ice jigging rods. The heartfelt joy of sharing days outside fishing with friends and family has created a lifetime of memories and lessons.

The stories I tell in this book are all true, including names. I clarified details of events with those present or with whom I shared that time and space, because memory does not always serve us perfectly and anglers tend to exaggerate their catch. While we joke that all anglers lie, and some resting places are actually named for us—such as The Liar's Bench—fish sizes, details, and fables of how they came to hand (or not) are true, to the best of my memory. I offer as little overstating as I can manage.

Most pictures in this book are taken with a cell phone. This is not professional photography, but has allowed me to capture some testimonials for telling my stories.

Finally, my father is a professional writer (eight books and countless articles) and photographer, who is well known in the outdoor writers' world of fishing and hunting. My mother edited all of his work and they have both been my advisors and supporters in this project. I asked myself, "Is it okay to ride on his coattails of success?" in this endeavor and the resounding answer was "Absolutely." It is my first serious writing effort and may pale in comparison to his, but with all I do in life, my parents have encouraged me to forge ahead and do it my way. I hope the reader finds some joy, self-identification, entertainment, and yes, emotional connection in my offering. Mostly, I wish you peace and solitude in all you do and, if you fish, may it bring you abundance.

Enjoy the read and *go fish!*

Sue Daignault
October 2023
Harpswell, Maine

A Full
Net

Chapter One
In the Genes

The ties that bind us.

My clan.

The tribe I grew up with.

The people who love me for who I am because they were part of the mold I came from.

This is my family. We fished together during all hours of the day and night, and we became awesome troubleshooters, problem solvers, and collaborators. We were intent on finding and catching fish.

Parents pass on physical characteristics, such as eye color, to their children through their genes. Our parents passed on a love of fishing to us. All of us in the Daignault (pronounced DAY-NO) clan have a knack for it, an innate connection that was likely learned but I like to think it's in our genes. The love of fishing was passed from my parents, Frank and Joyce, to all of us kids—older brother Dickie, older sister Carol, and my identical twin sister Sandy, who has been known to stop off to fish for speckled trout both to and from work, sometimes in a skirt.

It makes perfect sense to me that we would grow up and continue fishing whenever we can. Our early summers were spent

Fishing is in the genes, I tell you. Here's my mom holding a trout.

fishing. My parents and my three siblings fished the beaches of Rhode Island in my youngest years, and then we fished outer Cape Cod for striped bass and bluefish when I grew a little older. Dickie was four years older than me and Carol was a year and a half older. Sandra was three minutes younger than me and to this day I hold those three precious minutes over her head.

The story of how the genes combined to make us who we are must include the strength, beauty, and awesome love only a mother can provide. My mother, Joyce, is an amazing woman and more than our matriarch. She and Dad already had Dickie and Carol and were barely into their early twenties when Sandy and I were born. Mom developed her own career while mothering us, completed her master's degree, and became an excellent teacher. All the while she was the backbone of our family, and an exceptional outdoorswoman, keeping pace with Dad and the men who dominated the field. She is still revered today as an expert shooter and hunter. Those who fished alongside her when I was a kid saw her angling ability.

Spending entire summers keeping us all fed and cared for while living in our camper on Cape Cod could not have been easy

Sandy (right) and me on Cape Cod with some of the day's catch.

for her. While most of the time it was cozy and joyous, it could be challenging. Mom and Dad slept in a lower bunk equivalent to a full-sized bed. Carol and Sandy shared a bunk created when we put the camper's table down. Meanwhile, Dickie and I shared an overhead bunk. Together, Carol and Dickie were too big to share a single bunk so Sandy and I, both younger and smaller, were split up. If I had to pee in the night, I had to climb over Dickie trying not to wake him up, then lower myself five feet down to the lower bunk where Sandy and Carol were sleeping. Then I'd drop down to the floor. Dad often slept with his arm out in the aisle, and I was too small to climb over. He was also often awake and would grab me halfway by. The toilet was in the camper rear with a curtain. Actually, I always woke them all up!

There was a small propane gas stove that Mom used for cooking, and she was an amazing planner, carefully mapping out meals she could handle. Every few days we went into town to do laundry, get water, dump the septic tank, buy groceries, and sell our fish. Town days were fun and usually meant a trip to the candy

Me with my sister Carol.

store (when younger), pizza (and beer for the folks), and walks down Commercial Street in Provincetown while my parents sold the fish at the pier.

She did all of this between tides and likely on less sleep than any other mother out there. Her love for all of us has been unwavering and awesome. In retrospect, my mother was *super-human* to get it all done and fish as much as she did.

In his first book, *Twenty Years on the*

Dickie bringing in his catch.

Cape, Dad writes plenty about how we got here and why we all remain drawn to the outdoors and fishing in his dedication.

> For nearly all of the thirty-one years that my wife, Joyce, and I have been together, sportsmen of the beaches, gun clubs, and streams of New England have reminded me of how lucky I have been to have a wife beside me to share my sport. While I appreciate that this was never intended as an admonition, it has always made me uneasy to think that anyone might believe that I did not know what I had. Moreover, in their efforts to remind me of my enviable social wealth, they could never have known how

My dad—angler, teacher, writer, inspiration.

Mom. How she managed all of us every summer is still a mystery to me.

absolute the relationship remains. There is far more
to a marriage than having a partner that can shoot
grouse, fly cast, and haul great stripers from the high
surf. A wife from such a marriage would be able to
bear beautiful children, nurse him and those children
in a time of need, aid in his education, share in his
literary interests, and grieve in his disappointments.
In addition to being a lover and companion, such a
person would share in the production of one's books.

Anyone lucky enough to have such a wife and
who had to be reminded of that fortune, would be
unworthy.

To Joyce. My God, who else.

In the seventies and eighties we caught fish along the beaches
using rod and reel and sold our catches for money. And we were
crazy for it. It was hard work fishing into the night while playing
hard all day, as kids inevitably do. When Dad would pound on
the side of the camper announcing that the fish were in, we'd all
stumble out of our warm sleeping bags to answer the call. It was
like when I was later on a ship being called to general quarters; we
all showed up. It's what we did. We celebrated our victories when
the fish were plentiful and lamented our shortcomings when they
were not. We filled the coolers some nights and others, we got
skunked. I know if I asked each of my siblings today, they would
all say we had a blast running wild on the beaches of outer Cape
Cod as teens. I would also hear another truth—there were times
we were darn tired of fishing and living in a small camper all
summer with six people.

Today, as a woman with no children and blessed to still have
my parents and siblings around, I'd say I was darn fortunate. I
was breathing salt air, picking sand out of my toes, body tan and
hair blonde from summer sun. I was on a beach where I could

walk and run to my heart's content for miles. The sea was my daily bath and I got a freshwater rinse when I could get to the public showers that were miles down the beach. All summer Sandy and I were glued to one another laughing and playing. It was in my blood and my bones and now I want to fish whenever I can. As an adult, I miss doing it with all of them while we live our separate lives. I email fish pictures to them and they appease me with praise and delight. That's love.

All six of us fished together often, stringing out along a half mile or so of beach as we hop-scotched along, covering miles in a rising or falling tide. We would spread out and work an area of the beach, then pass the next one in line, mumbling "nothing" or "had a hit." We might stop and chat a bit before moving on. Six people doing this can cover some serious beach in a few hours. When we were done, it was clear there either *were* or *were not* fish in the area. When we hit them, we would fill all the coolers and only quit when we couldn't fit any more fish in the aisle of our camper. And then we headed straight for the fish pier to sell our catch. We weren't people who necessarily fished with friends back then, but we made buddies out there as we all came and went on the beaches. We were always on the move seeking fish.

While we were fishing, we used our flashlights to create SOS signals for anything from "I need help" to "catching fish" or "nothing happening." The flashlights were always at the ready in our pockets and Dad kept the batteries coming. Hey, it worked. Once, when my father accidentally put a gaff in his wrist on Nauset Beach, he used the buggy headlights to signal SOS and help came quickly to get him to medical care. He might have bled to death otherwise.

On one trip at a very young age in our beach buggy, we nearly lost Sandy. The day was hot, nearly one hundred degrees, and Dad warned us not to open the rear window. However, carbon monoxide poisoning was an abstract threat to us, so we

Me at sixteen with the biggest striper I've ever caught, a forty-seven pounder.

opened the window a little. When we got to Long Bar, we all bounced out of the back—except Sandy. Mom went to get her, and found her skin clammy and her breathing shallow. Dad grabbed her and raced her out into the fresh air. Dickie whimpered, sensing the fear rolling off our parents. Carol and I stood and stared. Mom and Dad began crying and praying.

Dad describes what happened next:

> It crossed my mind that my greed was at fault. Maybe that is where I was when her eyes opened and she began to cry. As long as I live I will never forget the fear that we all felt, nor the relief when our baby began to cry as she sipped Kool-Aid. Within minutes she was flopping around in a foot of water behind Long Bar with the others who watched her closely.

I don't remember the incident, but it is often recounted by my parents and Dickie, and it always brings tears to their eyes.

Sandy and I turned sixty in 2021. During the weeks before that milestone event, the thing I dreamed most about doing was meeting her on the water somewhere to share time, lament our missed days, catch up . . . and yes, *fish*; yelling and swearing after the ones that got away. With wisdom growing each passing year, I now see that fishing was a catalyst to build our relationship. I miss fishing with her so much.

I ask myself: "What's the great abiding draw to fishing?" It's an excuse for me to be outside, to feel the water compress the muscles in my legs, to let go of the day's troubles, to be free of worry, and to think about nothing at all or about everything. My mind is set free when I am water-bound, my heart is hopeful, and, yes, I long for that tug—the one that's an expectation, yet a surprise every time. Most fish are normal, small or regular in size and beauty, but then the fish of a lifetime hits and makes it even more special. It's an affirmation. Like life itself, it is full of long days and hours, mostly mundane, unless we take the time to appreciate the beauty. I consider every fish now a thing of magnificent glory and a gift. It is a sign I'm getting older and more attentive. I want to catch every moment and live like it could be the last. Another day begins that may or may not include a fish, but hope is restored.

Chapter Two

The Old Man and the Sea

The summer before Dad turned eighty, I wrote this article for *The Fisherman* magazine about him. My parents, both school teachers, have had an amazing and positive influence on who I have become, as a woman, wife, daughter, sister, friend, angler, and teacher. My dad also became a well-established author, while my mom edits every word as he plows ahead in his subsequent career as a writer and photographer. He gets the fanfare, but she is right there by his side.

Born November 14, 1936, it's time for Dad— more commonly known as Frank Daignault to the readers of *The Fisherman*—to turn eighty. It's fitting that he was born in late fall, during the height of hunting and fishing seasons. He says he didn't begin fishing until he was seven, but I think he must have had a little fishing rod and rifle in the womb with Memere. His passion for fishing and hunting took off and he shared it with all of us, as well as with his many readers along the way.

Dad began writing in 1969 when I was just eight; he got his first decent camera a few years later, and has written eight books, including *Twenty Years on the Cape, Striper Hot Spots, Eastern Tides, Striper Hot Spots Second Edition, The Trophy Striper, Striper Hot Spots-New England, Fly Fishing The Striper Surf, Striper Hot Spots-Mid Atlantic,* and *Striper Surf.* His countless magazine articles have appeared in renowned publications such as *Saltwater Sportsman* where he began and continues to this day for *The Fisherman* (since 1977), *Surfcaster's Journal,* and others. He manages an online blog at StriperSurf. com where he has frequent conversations with avid fishermen and shares the knowledge he has acquired over the years with them. He also has done radio interviews, and for many years has spoken at fishing shows. For much of his eighty years, Frank Daignault

Sandy and me at age four, fierce fishers even then.

has been an avid angler, sharing his love of the sport along the way with the readers of *The Fisherman*, outdoor sports seminars, and fishing clubs. I attend these now as an avid angler, guide, and fly fishing instructor, often running into people who know my father, follow his writing and want to know the inside scoop on the family. We never were ones to give away our fishing hot spots and were even known to lie about where the fish were!

This brings to mind a short—but true—story that Dad just loves to tell . . . According to his recollections it goes something like this: We were regularly fishing the beaches of Cape Cod and the folks from away would come and often ask how the fishing was. We were instructed to always say it wasn't very good, so in unison Sandy and I replied like a couple of songbirds saying, "There's no fish here." But then one of the guys asked, "What are they not hitting on?" and again we simultaneously and emphatically responded, "Webels." Who could ever disbelieve two cute identical twins singing to a tune like that? We may as well have been saying, "The fish are here!" I don't think we were alone fishing that night.

Sandy and I still smile over that one and so many other times we were partners in crime and fishing. Like the time I visited her in Louisiana when I was on Coast Guard duty. It was after the big BP oil spill and I was sent for sixty days to help out; all I could think of was bull red and speck fishing with my sister, only three minutes younger than I. During those two months I ate fish most nights with lunches of peanut butter and jelly sandwiches. The seventy-two dollar per diem was saved to pay for weekend guides to go fishing and I went six times over those two months. But the best was the haul with Sandy when we made our guide so green from the work we put him through; even the two hundred dollar tip didn't appease that poor man for the fileting he had when we were done! His final words were, "You !*$#@&^ girls can fish!" So you see, Mom and Dad made us this way and it's all their fault, but there are worse things I could be addicted to, eh?

I could spend many pages getting into so many fishing stories, and share countless pictures of the big fish caught, but it's the intense love of the sport and gift that Dad has given that matters most to me. His innate ability to put pen to paper and tell his many stories is what you readers see, but I see a man who loves me with his entire heart and taught me to do something I love. I go fishing any time I can.

I recently asked Dad for a list of all the fish he has tightened a line for over the years and he gave me the following: striped bass, bluefish, mackerel, catfish, perch (yellow and white), smallmouth bass, largemouth bass, pickerel, landlocked salmon, sea run browns, salter brook trout, white shad, cusk, eel, cod, pollock, fluke, scup, sculpin, goosefish, dogfish, and tautog. I bet he has forgotten some, but that's quite a list!

Now we all know that behind every successful man is a fabulous woman, right? Mom and Dad celebrated their sixtieth anniversary in January 2017. She reads his work before it ever leaves the house (electronically now, of course), but it's more than that. Her love, support, strength, perseverance, and

A bit older, but still double-trouble fishing twins!

sense of humor have been the glue of our family and will forever remain in our hearts.

The Daignault tribe of Dickie, Carol, Sandy, and I all have a knack for fishing, and that's putting it lightly. We spent summers on Cape Cod as kids, and really had a ball on the beaches. With sand in our toes and salt in our hair we became blond and tan in the sun daily while fishing many nights together. We built our love for the sport but more for each other. We bonded closely yet learned solitude and independence, then grew up and went separate ways. We take life by the horns and hold on tight, the way Mom and Dad taught us to do.

Today, fishing brings me to many awesome places that are very different from the ones I saw growing up. I never knew what a bonefish was or

17

how to stalk them on the flats of the tropics, but the passion I picked up remains and the fishing brings me solace. I still angst for the heart-throbbing surprise that always accompanies a striper strike and daily catches in Maine are now posted on Facebook with friends as "The Catch Of The Day."

Dad's father, Pepere, left us at fifty-nine, when Sandy and I were just a week old. His only brother passed away at sixty-four so let's be candid: none of us expected he'd live to eighty. He's here and continues to enjoy skeet and trap shooting and hunting for pheasant, turkey, and deer. Mom and Dad like to fly fish at the local club and bother some trout in the hard water of winter. He's still writing, still talking fishing. You know when fishermen are lying right? Their lips are moving!

We love you Dad. Happy 80th. Let's have a few more!

I had no idea that nearly five years later I would attempt to write my first book, and I now hope to finish it while he and Mom are around to see it, enjoy reading it and be proud of me. (Yes, we all want our parents to be proud.)

I share many of my ongoing fishing pictures with him because his first and strongest recommendation to me has been to have pictures to include and accentuate the stories. In these days of cell phones and internet use we can shoot pictures of each other, take selfies even when alone, and document just about anything, anytime, and anywhere. I have over four thousand pictures on my current phone and many of them are taken using the self-timer mode because I am often alone or not standing near another person when I catch fish. I post almost daily shots of fish caught by me or friends and can throw a story together most weeks based on something that happened on the water.

My parents had a strong influence on the extraordinarily gifted life I have been given. This is something I am grateful for each and every day. Mom's impact has been steadfast and runs across all aspects of my life. Dad's as well, and little did he know that giving me fishing would actually make me so much better— the fun, escape, solitude, and recovery helps me to relocate my heart and recenter, time and time again.

Chapter Three
Heartbreak

I fish through winters now. Maybe it's a sign of my age (I'm in my early sixties) or an advancement of my addictive personality, but I don't want to lose a day. I recently had such an uncanny string of events that they could only have occurred through a combination of skill, local knowledge of rivers, and simple Christmas magic! It was December 2020 in Maine. There were no leaves left on the trees and temperatures were in the forties, but it felt like thirty with the brisk wind. My wading shoes were snug around two layers of poly liners under wool socks with toe warmers in place. I wore my favorite fishing ball cap covered by a wool hat my mom knitted for me, along with the matching wool mittens. I can't fish with mittens on, but they stayed in my pockets for intermittent warm-ups, the only thing that kept me on the river long enough to be productive. A thermos of hot black coffee was always in my vest as well, a lifeblood that kept my icy insides warm and a tad jittery. It wasn't comfortable fishing most days, but it was doable. Most anglers, by that time of year, have stowed gear for the quarter of the year when open season is closed and only the year-round rivers are left to fish in Southern Maine. The rivers tend not to freeze and stocked fish remain catchable for hardy souls willing to dredge nymphs through icy waters and hope. Not feeling your toes for a few hours is a fairly common winter ailment.

Up until three years ago, I packed it in from December to March like everyone else. At the time, I spent a night per week working in the fishing store of L.L. Bean, where I learned of the open year-round fisheries. In studying the list of the state's rivers that were open, I found most were in Southern Maine where temperatures are a bit warmer and the moving water keeps areas from freezing over. One of those rivers was just thirty minutes from home.

This story actually starts out in heartbreak. I traveled an hour to a Southern Maine river to meet Bri Dostie, a woman who is now a friend of mine, but was simply an acquaintance at the time. Bri and I knew of each other and met briefly a year or two earlier in a fly casting class I was running, but we really didn't know each other. Bri is one of the sweetest souls you could ever meet and I really liked her. She also is an excellent fly fisher. We connected on Facebook and hatched our plan to meet. We decided to give the tailwater near the mouth of this estuary a shot, hoping for a possible stray sea-run trout or really any trout since late fall and early winter fishing can get considerably slow. The meeting was more about seeing each other, establishing possible future connections, and learning our way around this river, something we both wanted to do. The tide was halfway out when we arrived and she knew the area well enough to know wading access was safe. I had no idea, but I had driven by the place a few times and seen anglers in the river. Excited to finally see both Bri and a river I knew had a decent reputation, I sped south down the highway like a teen heading to a beach party.

We made our way around the river for a few hours, sort of together, but apart, the way anglers do. We checked in here and there, shared coffee and flies, shared notes about a possible tug or two that may actually have been the bottom, and then we separated again to keep searching. We were complacent and happy simply to be outside rather than getting more screen time than our eyes, butts, and heads needed. I settled into a nice little run along the embankment just downstream from her, thinking, "Well, isn't this a nice little hole for a fish to hang out in." It was shallow all the way across the river to reach the run, but then dropped into a small, five-foot deep channel that was clear, bronze, and dark. It was as fishy as it gets and right against the river's left bank. I could have walked in my hikers from the shore and hit this spot easier, but was already in the water.

On my second short cast into this channel along the river's edge my line held up hard on the bottom, or so I thought. As I stripped in slack, that bottom started to bounce and move to the right, down river; I knew immediately I was on to a better-than-average fish. Bri saw my rod doubled over and yelled "Whoa!" I think she made her way toward me, like a good guide, sensing I was into something meaningful. My shoulder had been tender for weeks so I was sporting only a seven-foot ten-inch L.L. Bean Pocketwater, a five-weight outfit, and I promptly wished I had a bigger stick. It's a great little rod, mind you, "little" and soft—meaning it bends easily. My drag was on the lighter side so I slipped my hand to the knob to make it a tad tighter, careful not to move it much with a 5x tandem rig trailing my only big white wooly bugger. My good friend and guide Kate taught me about the value of tandem rigs (using two flies on one line), doubling your fish chances (and hang ups), I had been experiencing suc-cess. Various thoughts plowed through my fish-brain as I began planning how to chase, not chase, cross the channel, not cross the channel, get the fish to a decent landing pad . . . but the most pressing one was "Oh-my-God, I have 5x tippet, maybe four-pound breaking strength and this is a better-than-your-average trout on." At this point I didn't know whether the fish had hit the bugger on 1x leader or the soft hackle in tow on flimsy 5x tippet (basically, the leader and tippet are used to connect the fishing line to the fishing fly).

The fish ran downstream about twenty feet and my drag provided just the right pressure. Then it came back up to the hole where he had initially tackled my tandem rig and held up on the bottom as I told Bri this was no small fish. I was still in the middle of the river, inside of the channel and made the decision to cross it from below up to my waist while she took a position across from me with net in hand. Her net was one with a longer handle than mine, but she could not reach where my fish was stubbornly resting, contemplating his next move. He had hunkered down on the bottom. We couldn't see him, but knew where the line led directly below while I peered down to see anything I could. Several times she asked if I was sure it was a fish and I explained rocks don't run downstream. Then he made another run in the same direction so I kept moderate pressure, fearing the 5x tippet to the soft hackle would snap if I horsed him. He then made the same move back to his hold in the channel. I had never been held to the bottom like this by a big trout, but had read about the behavior being common with larger fish. By now I was armed with my net and up to my elbows in icy water trying to reach down into that hold because he wasn't budging.

His final move was a slow rise up and downriver, so I raised my little rod to keep the line tight without a lot of pressure. You see, fish are more patient than anglers and he'd rubbed my tippet on a rock; that final move was my demise. It broke two inches below my knot, where the 5x soft hackle had been tied to the bend of the bugger. I watched his deep orange flank swim past me down river while the mega wooly bugger remained dangling on my line. Repeating the expletives Bri and I simultaneously shouted would be unladylike and only something routinely uttered by sailors. Then I held my breath in, sat on a rock, and with all my might tried not to break that five-weight over my knee as Bri said, "Don't do it, Sue."

I breathed in.

I breathed out.

She waited, not making a sound, just watching for the angst to leave my face, I'm sure. She was smart and experienced enough to know nothing would help as we waited in silence for the pain to subside. Five or six minutes passed, an eternity, as the wind returned to my sails, the cursing and recount of what had happened returned with my exhale. I promised I was done fishing forever and ever, but we know that didn't happen. She asked if I was okay, my reply simply a grunt by now. I took several more casts in that channel knowing it was over, hoping that big brookie would forget about me and come back to hunker down again. We know that didn't happen either.

I have experienced the aforementioned overwhelming desire to break a rod, akin to chucking a golf club into the pond after an awful game-breaking shot (I suck at golf so who cares). The temporary grief of losing the fish of a lifetime, or perceived fish of a lifetime (since we don't really know what was on the line), can be heartbreaking, but we get over it. Maybe it was a rock that moved with orange paint down the side. I say, just let go, swear it off, yell, even cry, take a few breaths, and get back in the water. I quickly moved into the vital "acceptance" stage, my fish-brain analyzing the disaster and what I may have done wrong—horsed him too hard on a five-weight rod with a light tippet, or underestimated his size, or, and finally, I needed a long-handled, larger net!

Bri and I continued fishing, scouting further upriver, and never had another touch. I lamented about that fish a few times while Bri patiently nodded and affirmed my crazy. She got it. When we parted later in the day, I thanked her for understanding as we agreed the day was more about togetherness, getting outside, and stomping new grounds. I would never be the same. When we ice fished the following winter, she referred to that fish as "the unnamed fish that we won't talk about!" Ouch. We laughed this time but the pain of the loss returned. On the ice we landed only a few small, ten-inch brookies, with some dropped, but no one got their heart broken.

On the way home from that loss, a half hour north of the location I'd been with Bri, I couldn't help stopping at the river where I had landed a twenty-three-inch brown the day before, wanting to feel such elation again. Maybe it was revenge, I don't know. Number Two Big Brown was special because he made me forget about the heartbreaker earlier in the day. He was a rebound fish. I was shocked I could lose and land a monster on the very same day, on two rivers and very different conditions. The emotional scale was pegged out!

I am going back to that river, soon, hopefully to meet Bri and she knows darn well what we're after. She can do it—doesn't have to be me, but one of us needs to catch that fish or one a lot like it. I'd guess that was a two-foot brook trout and it was hooked in the mouth, not foul hooked. I saw enough to know that much with certainty. I know I need to accept that loss and that anything like that isn't likely to be repeated because that's fishing—we're out there every day and every hook up is different. The same water never passes by us again so each step in the river, each cast touches different parts and likely different fish.

Fishing heartbreak isn't unique to Maine. We've all had our hearts broken again and again. I had another one in Key West. I can only tell the short version as I'm just not over it yet, since my last telling of the story very recently left me sleepless and crazy. I was with a guide who was excellent. We had "floaters," large permit floating in a deep channel feeding, so he tied on a floating crab imitation to skid across the salty surface. I did as he instructed, casting sixty or seventy feet to their location with a back cast in heavy wind, tip down, at the ready. We had follows but they only licked my crab. Finally my very astute guide became more agitated and announced, "He's on it, get ready, strip, strip, strip—he's taking it!" Then all hell broke loose. He took it. I kept my rod tip down and stripped hard—the permit booked and as the slack line followed him, I got hold of it and held too tight, a novice move. I felt the weight of a very nice fish, estimated to be about twenty-five pounds by my heartbroken guide, as I refused to let him run and duly broke off the twenty-pound leader. Yup, gone . . . like a bad country song, gone. I think we both cried. I don't know if I can try again. I need more time on this one. These things take time to move on from.

I really do almost always think I am going to catch fish, but like any human, I have been so dejected at times I swear off fishing forever. When the pain of a big loss passes and we realize it's just the nature of fishing to catch and to lose fish, we remember that the point of being there really isn't even about the fishing. It offers an opportunity to escape the difficulties of life, our complicated minds, and excessive thinking, which can be exhausting. The water cleans the hard drive and forces me into starting over or at least stopping wherever my mind has been. It's just me, my comrades (if I am with somebody), fly choices, conditions, details, surroundings, fish, catching, releasing, and yes, sometimes losing. We may be after that tug and know we want to land the big one but if we get too fixated on the goal, loss will result more than gain because there are plenty of outings where no fish is touched at all.

Thank goodness time eases all pain, even heartbreak.

Chapter Four

Don't Shoot
the Cheeks!

For college, I chose to attend the United States Coast
Guard Academy. My father served in the Navy for a few years.
My brother, Dickie, served in the Coast Guard, but neither of
them were an influence on my decision. I was sure I was going to
college and I looked at all the service academies in high school.
The greatest influence on me was watching the Coast Guard
work on the beaches as we fished. I also really liked that their
missions were more humanitarian than military—saving lives,
protecting the environment, responding to emergencies, and
more. I remember one incident in Massachusetts. A small plane
crashed just off the beach in front of our camper. It carried a
father and son. The surf was rough and Coasties (this is a proper
term of endearment for us) came and launched a small boat in the
rough surf, pushed out, and got them. All of the campers turned
on their headlights to light the way for them. We cried. The
father died, but the son survived.

Once admitted, I attempted to break every rule they created
to teach us order and discipline, something I was also raised on,
but resisted much of the way. Suffice it to say, I made it through

in the four years prescribed, but not unscathed. I graduated with a bachelor's degree in marine engineering and an officer's commission as an ensign. I was required to complete a two-year tour at sea, and a five-year commitment to stay in the service.

On May 18, 1983, I was elated to be free and would soon head to Kodiak, Alaska, to serve my first tour of duty on *Firebush*, a 180-foot buoy tender homeported in one of the best fishing villages God could conjure up. It was perfect. Because I had majored in marine engineering, I had been expected to take an engineering billet on "billet night" when First Class Cadets (seniors, or "Firsties") pick (or take what's left) their first assignment upon graduation. We all had to serve two years at sea.

I cannot recall my billet number, but I was not in the upper half of my class. After being an A-student in high school, this was an "about face" for me. Yet, I was happy to get through, earn my bachelor's degree, and have a job for five years. Surprising everyone, I took a deck billet in Kodiak, half-thinking the fishing would at least be good, although that was not one of the endorsed criteria for billet choices. The alternatives were not palatable and may have been New York and the Gulf Coast, none of which did anything for me. (Had I known about redfishing at the time I may have gone to the Gulf, but that presented itself later in life.)

After graduation, I spent two weeks in England and Scotland traveling on a Brit-rail pass with my buddies, Lurilla and Jean. The journey included many pints, youth hostels, and touring around like the free birds we felt like after four years under the pressing academic, physical, and disciplinary standards of the academy. We had a blast and parted company back in the states, wishing each other all the best. I packed my possessions to set off for Alaska. In my bag was my first fly rod, a Fenwick that my girlfriends at the Academy chipped in to send me off with.

I met my ship after being air dropped onto an island in the Aleutian chain from an HH-52, a Coast Guard helicopter.

The boatswain's mate was there to toss me into the helicopter's Stokes litter (widely used in search and rescue for vertical recovery operations), strongly recommending (because enlisted do not give orders to officers, even if that officer is a very green ensign) that I keep all four paws inside the basket. Turns out the very same boatswain's mate would be the hero who gaffed my halibut later in this story. The helicopter brought me from Kodiak to the unnamed island and before I knew which was the pointy or square end, I was escorted to *Firebush*, an Iris-class buoy tender. My first watch onboard was that night, exhausted and a tad bruised up from my all-too-bumpy arrival.

I was the first woman ever assigned to the *Firebush*. There also were fifty-five men aboard. Numerous lessons presented themselves, including "don't make the guys cut out their skin flicks." Meaning, some nights the guys watched either porn movies or movies with plenty of scantily clad women. I don't know, I never stayed. One night I had the watch from eight to midnight, and went to the mess deck for a coffee, stumbling right into one of these movie events. I stopped to observe the screen while about thirty of the Coast Guard's finest took a collective breath. One of them whispered just loudly enough, "Shut it off, it's Ensign D." The screen went blank, but I knew what was up by that point. I acted like I hadn't seen a thing and loudly ordered, "Carry on gentlemen." Today, I'm not sure I agree with how I handled that situation, but at the time, I decided I would rather be accepted as part of the crew instead of claiming my seat as their one and only woman onboard. Heck, maybe I should even have sat down with them, but moving on seemed wise. Those guys became my brothers, looking out for me during port calls on the outer Aleutian Islands, when I joined them in hunting parties. I went ashore when I could to steal some exercise, while they kept "bear watch" and, well, we fished together. I came to really care for them and am proud today to call them shipmates. They treated

31

me respectfully and like their little sister. We were there to protect others and they protected me.

In my two years assigned to *Firebush,* I fished in Kodiak often, mostly with a spinning rod. I had the Fenwick, but I had no idea how to fly fish. There were all species of salmon around the island, but I recall only catching pink, chums, silvers, Dolly Varden, and trout. We used medium-sized rods and lures of differing colors as the salmon crammed into the rivers for the fall spawn run. It was wild and fun and I knew a few other women who also liked to hike and fish. Karen, my partner, and I officially got together in September 1984 when she came to Kodiak on a one-way ticket with only a few bags. One day we hiked to Hidden Lakes, which we swore were too shallow to hold fish, but we caught rainbows. We swam and fished in our bras and underwear because it was an unusually warm day in Kodiak, and who would have thought to bring a swimsuit? I recall on another trip catching my limit of two silver salmon from a kayak and canning multitudes of salmon to take with us later. There was a news story about a woman landing a four-hundred-pound halibut off of a dock in downtown Kodiak. Alas, it was not me!

I loved fishing on long summer days when the sun barely set, leaving the night sky dusky right through to morning. The winters were long, cold, and dark, with dusk hitting mid-afternoon and twelve-hour sleeps not uncommon. Some days I was so exhausted that I'd hit my Lily Lake pad and crash from six p.m. to six a.m. For anyone into hunting or fishing, it was our salvation and a gift from heaven, although we paid a high price to live there and work on the ship. Nevertheless, I wouldn't trade that tour for the world.

Officers were usually assigned in pairs to share a stateroom on ships, but being the only female on *Firebush* I had a stateroom to myself. I was a mere ensign, arriving at twenty-two years old in June 1983, sporting the same rank as all United States Coast Guard Academy graduates. I had one thick stripe on each petite

I caught this huge halibut in 1985 while serving with the Coast Guard in Alaska. Karen and I ate this this fish for a year!

shoulder that was twice as thick as that of a Firstie. That stripe was one quarter of the total I would retire with thirty years later, and I never saw it coming. I was alone on a ship of men, working my ass off, drinking too much when we got ashore, and trying to become something. I had no idea what. I met the qualifications to be assigned as the ship's navigator and operations officer (Ops Boss) about eighteen months into that two-year tour. The Old Man (commanding officer) would routinely come up to the bridge and light his pipe, knowing the watch would be sick in minutes from the combination of smoke and wave action. We all puked and carried on. We planned our navigational aid work based on our orders, but we always finished off our days in fishing hot spots. We needed just the right depth for halibut, or "barn doors," as we labeled the big ones. It quickly became clear they'd chosen the right woman for the job when it came to being the ship's navigator, Ops Boss, and leading angler, because I got us to those fishing holes on time and under budget every chance I could. The commanding officer being a fisherman helped immensely so he approved of my antics so long as the work was completed first. No problem, skipper!

We hung large cast masters and tins over the side on bait-casters or large spinning rods, jigging with one elbow resting on the thick gunwale. The effective method was to free-spool to the bottom, then raise the jig just a bit and punch it hard by pushing down on the rod butt while the elbow acted as a fulcrum on the gunwale. A hard punch of about two feet would pop the jig up from the bottom enticing the halibut to hit. "Chicken halibut" were small in size and very good to eat, but we were all after the barn doors. When they hit, we'd set hard with everything we had and they'd feel like a live barn door on the line. A Coastie could feed his or her family for a year on one of these fish. Once to the surface, the boatswain would shoot the monster in the head, always careful as we'd yell "don't hit him in the cheeks!" or the filet mignon portion of the fish. This sounds cruel, but knowing we were keeping legal fish to eat, it was the safest way for those onboard—a fish weighing a hundred pounds or more, flopping wildly on deck, could hurt anyone it came near.

In June 1985 I had two weeks left in my two-year tour on the ship. On a clear, beautiful night somewhere out on the Aleutian Islands—I truly do not recall our exact location—a handful of the guys were on deck fishing, smoking, and chatting. I got off watch at eight p.m., exhausted, hungry, over-caffeinated, and ready to fish. A few were being caught at the anchorage I had chosen a few hours prior, in just the right amount of water, and in the perfect halibut hunting grounds. We were in the right place, I could feel it. Soon my baitcaster doubled over with a barn door and I hauled back with all the 150 pounds I think I weighed at the time. Guys on either side of me reeled in sharply to make way for what would be an epic battle, cheering me on. I fought like a true sailor while the skipper had me by the waist, his pipe burning hot in his teeth and blowing smoke in my face, pinning us both to the buoy deck, while he bellowed, "Hang on, lieutenant, hang on!" The two of us were dragged several times to the gunwale and my leg went up to keep my arms from getting jammed against it.

Several times he offered to take my rod, but I respectfully replied, "No f-ing way, skipper, sir!" He chuckled a lot and knew that would be an insistent "no way" any day of the week. The boatswain did his job and shot my halibut mercifully just before the boat hook brought the brute on deck and I became the first female member of the *Firebush* Charters, Inc., One Hundred Pound Plus Club. My fish weighed 152 pounds. I shared the pair of fat cheeks with the boatswain that night in celebration of our feat as we laughed about the lifelong bruises he inflicted the day he picked me up on that island in the Stokes litter. Karen and I ate that fish for a year. This awesome catch so near the end of my time on that ship capped it all off.

It turns out that boatswain was one of the finest Coasties and gentlemen I have met in my Coast Guard career. The guys were allowed to have facial hair then, and he had a thick red beard. He was short and stout but solid. He barked orders like a bulldog and kept the deck crew in line through some pretty harrowing situations from cleaning cruddy buoys and anchors pulled up from the deep to hanging over the side to gaff huge halibut with his boat hook. He was also the man who gaffed a very large Japanese glass ball for me in ten-foot rollers, while the Old Man was fast asleep and I had the watch. These glass floats are popular collector's items now and we looked for them in the water while underway. They were once used by fishermen in many parts of the world to keep their fishing nets, longlines or drop lines, afloat. Since I had the watch and spotted the thing, it was mine but the boatswain's mate third class had the deck watch and did the heavy lifting. He was crude, yet a gentleman, funny, and kind. By the end of my tour we were close, although I don't think he had been fond of a woman joining his ship when I was first assigned. Maybe fishing bonded us. Maybe we were just kindred spirits. I still have the glass ball today.

———

Two years on any ship isn't easy work. And being the only woman on one offers additional challenges. I was alone the first year and seemed to work all of the time. However, as an outdoorswoman and avid angler, it was an awesome tour and Kodiak was an awesome place to see and live. I may never have experienced the area or the fishing had I not made that unexpected choice on billet night at the Academy. I'd like to go back some time to see how it has changed and experience fishing as a better angler.

CHAPTER FIVE
HOME TURF

Anglers can be a secretive lot, not usually open or even truthful about where we fish, how we fish, what we use, or when. I grew up in an environment where if we shared where we were catching many fish, we were never alone again. Since we were fishing commercially at the time—surfcasting for stripers on Cape Cod—keeping our hot spots a secret was vital to our continued success. Early in life it became ingrained in me not to tell others where I was catching fish. Tell anyone where and when you're catching fish and multitudes would converge upon that spot before you even arrive.

I belong to several online groups that openly share and help others get out and find the fish, including specifics on how to access places, what to use, and how to rig up. They are women's fishing groups so maybe I am more motivated to share with my fellow fly sisters. We openly educate and support one another in techniques and places, and we even organize groups of women getting together to fish. There is safety in numbers and some women feel more comfortable trekking around the woods and waters with others. No offense to the guys, but women face more safety issues out there than men do. One group is United Women

37

The admin team for the online group United Women on the Fly.

on the Fly, a closed women's fly-fishing group on Facebook. If I don't want to post where I am fishing, I simply tell women to send me a private message, and then I share it. The second group is Maine Women Fly Fishers (MWFF). This is the Maine women's chapter of Trout Unlimited; it is not a closed group, so anyone can access it online. I don't openly share where I am fishing in this group because anyone out there can show up to the locations I identify. I see that as a safety issue, so again, I go to a private message format.

Karen and I have lived in Harpswell, Maine, for twenty-four years. We live in a sixty-year-old simple ranch with three bedrooms and two baths on three acres, strategically placed on tidal water where striped bass swim daily between May and October! We walk down forty stairs to our dock where our motorboat and kayaks stay in season. We bought the house in 1999 and have renovated parts of it over the years. Before that, we lived in

Topsham, just ten miles away, but fishing really took off for me when we moved to this wonderful waterfront location. Karen isn't really into fishing, but she supports my affliction, often playing boat captain to bring me to favorite fishing spots.

One motivator for living here is its tranquil nature, with less than five thousand year-round residents, half of whom are snow-birds, making winters quiet and quaint. It consists of a peninsula, three large islands (Great, Orr's, Bailey), more than two hundred smaller islands, and boasts 216 miles of coastline. Industries here once included farming, ship building, and fishing, while lobster-ing and clamming remain a thriving part of our economy. It's no secret that a major reason I love it here is the annual migration of striped bass. I mean you can pull up on any coastal Maine location, southern beaches or harbors, and likely pick up stripers if you have half a clue, but the ease of them literally swimming right by our place makes it doubly lovely. I had my share of logis-tical nightmares in the Coast Guard so simply hanging a dozen rigged fly rods, spin rods, and baitcasters in the garage armed and ready for action is quite convenient. Whenever I can, I roll out barely awake and stumble into fifty-degree water in late May and continue that routine right into October. Riding the tides and hugging the eastern coastline, stripers head northward as I lie in wait for their arrival each year. It's a recurring ritual to gear up, watch their movement and be prepared for their on-time arrival.

After we moved to Harpswell in May, it didn't take me long to learn the tides, moon phases, and other conditions that make certain secret spots the best places to catch striped bass when they migrate north from the Chesapeake Bay area. I now follow the migration online so I can time when to meet them at the New Hampshire border or southern Maine beaches, especially if I'm feeling too anxious to wait for them to arrive in Harpswell Sound. Most years I have simply awaited the arrival to our backyard, beginning to stretch lines with a few casts as soon as they get to the Pott's Point latitude. Within a few days of knowing they are in my coastal region, I find them in the sound with my kayak, our motorboat, off our dock, or by simply wading nearby. The magic water temperature seems to be right at fifty degrees when they arrive, as per my twenty-plus years of logs. Fifty degrees in the water and topside can be nippy after a few hours standing in it so there are many "test" sessions just to keep the place honest and mark their arrival. Arrival to our dock is generally in late May while departure is too soon in early October, but I keep swearing to go join them some time on their migration, in one direction or the other.

I believe the fish are in most of the desirable spots throughout the coastal region once the migration is complete. Specifics then become well-kept secrets among anglers but are often dependent on the wind, moon, and tide. My preference is for overcast days, especially those with heavy rain. The more uncomfortable it is for humans out there, the better the fishing is. Striped bass are nocturnal so they feed more at night, but I have a job and like to sleep at night, so I tend to fish dusk and dawn and a lot during overcast days. I will even fish on bright and sunny summer days and catch some decent fish, but the best results come at night. My father often chides me to get out there late at night, but I just don't do it often; I can catch fish during more reasonable times of the day and still live a relatively sane lifestyle. I love the quarter moon tides, or those a few days before the full and new moons with a noon and midnight high tide. I am not fond of the actual full moon other than for the awesome view on the water. The bright nights and higher tides with mega water levels and stronger current just seem to put off the fish for a few days around it. However, a nine or ten a.m. or p.m. incoming tide with its full flood at five or six a.m. or p.m. is just right for me to fish and still get a good night's sleep. I think that probably works well for just about any beach or jetty location, too, but getting to know a specific area is half the fun. Of course, for every statement I make about when I find fish, I can name another time and tide when I have come up empty—they may just be sitting out there all day every day for all I know.

Because I grew up surfcasting, I am most comfortable standing in the water in waders or even board shorts once things warm up. I recall one morning landing a dozen schoolies on my seven-weight fly rod at dawn in pouring rain, in less than an hour. It was just a blast. One summer day I invited my friend, Nome, and a friend of hers, Tina, to give it a go. It poured buckets that day, so hard the clay bottom was stirred up, muddying the shoreline; it seemed unfishable, but we caught fish. I have no idea how the fish even saw our flies in those conditions, but they hit as if it was crystal clear. My greatest success in Harpswell has been standing in the water or even casting off our dock on warm summer evenings with friends, sharing a soft drink and

Karen isn't really into fishing, but she often serves as captain to bring me to my favorite spots.

catching up. The kayak and boat offer opportunities to hit other places around the sound to find other sea creatures and wildlife, from porpoises and seals to seagulls, cormorants, eagles, osprey, sandpipers, kingfishers, and so much more. I admit that taking a boat ride means I am calculating the tide and which area would be right to hit when we pass by. Karen, my boat captain, knows that and appeases me as long as we can look for wildlife, too, and bring cookies and coffee, so we please both of us and have favorite routes to check out.

We have given local favorite spots names that have nothing to do with where they are or what their real names may be. One is the Honey Hole, coined for my having one exceptional summer just a half mile away and perfect at the high slack tide. I have a neighbor who lives on Honey Hole and with permission I could just cast from her yard, but for some reason it is best casting to shore from the middle of the sound. After studying it on the moon low where I could see, within the flat, the hole that attracted fish. I knew it would turn out to be a fine place to fish. I took Kate there once in the fall and we watched breaking fish come through the Honey Hole while anchored offshore from it, trying not to scare the school. After a few casts with fly rods she grabbed her spinner and had this very ugly plug on, the Pink Lady. I said, "Kate, what the heck is that pink thing? They aren't gonna hit that!" She proceeded to prove me wrong. Pink is now my favorite color for stripers! Fish came through there for an hour on each side of the high slack, breaking and hitting our Pink Ladies and we laughed ourselves silly. My favorite striper candy is a deep pink single hook, Albie Snack, that a fishing buddy gave me years ago. When they're ignoring white, light pink or anything else, the deep pink turns them on.

The Point is also a half-mile away and only accessible to me by boat or kayak because I'd have to trespass through someone's property to reach it. My favorite thing for the years here has been

Me with Kate Farnam—friend, guide, and fantastic angler.

to paddle or pedal a kayak to this secret location, land the boat, and cast from the rocks into the rip on a dropping tide. I once landed our thousand-pound motorboat on those rocks and the tide dropped out while I was busy fishing, completely distracted. It wasn't easy prying the boat from that high and dry position back into the water. I would often return in the dark after a perfect dropping sunset tide, while Karen waited on the dock with a flashlight signaling me back in the fog; well, it seems perfect at one and a half to two and a half hours down on the dropping tide, but the timing has varied over the years. Again, having seen the area at low tide I can surmise exactly why fish likely stop off there on the edge of the ledge, just below the underside of the water-covered rocks, with bait passing above. Like magic, they seem to be there more times than not. They're often deep and I do best with a sinking lure or fly and risk having a lunker take me to the bottom to rub off the hook, or worse, break off the line. I know fish aren't rational creatures but they sure know how to lose you if there are rocks or objects in the area. That's why the big ones often seem to get away. They're big for a reason!

Monster Alley got its name after I landed a forty-two-inch lunker from my kayak. I have only caught a few fish there over the years but it is several miles away and not a short paddle. Pott's Point is the actual name of another place with several fishy nooks and crannies that hold fish at all levels of the tide. My problem with that place is I once fell on rocks laden with seaweed and thought I fractured my arm. When I finally got up, seeing stars from the pain, I swore I was done there. The incoming tide can sneak up on you and make your return to solid land difficult and wet. The rocky shoreline along Cedar Beach on Bailey's Island has been known to produce many nice fish, but access in a rolling sea can be precarious and unsafe. And so I don't forget to say it, as a career retired Coast Guard officer, always wear your personal floatation device (PFD, or life vest) in a kayak or motorboat, leave a float plan as to where you're going and when you expect to return, and take a cell phone. Brightly colored jackets, hats, boats, etc., always help for spotting you before or after an emergency. Remember there may not be a cell signal everywhere you go, so how to get help in an emergency is a necessary question to answer. A VHF radio is never a bad idea.

There are a few other secret spots and self-coined names I have adopted here but some things just need to remain unknown. Most anglers can be dodgy and secretive, holding their favorite spots near and dear, sharing their precise locations with only the closest of buddies. Others, we may blindfold to get them to the spot, or run them in a few circles en route so they've no idea where they really are. Many know if they can get on the water or to the shoreline without trespassing they can probably locate fish because fish travel coastwise foraging for food. Sightings of birds working are telltale signs of actively feeding fish. Ultimately, the tides dictate the daily rhythm of fish location and movement, at least in my experience.

My general rule is to respect no trespassing postings and locate the public access points to the water I'd like to fish. I also link up with people who know an area and can safely guide me on the water. Checking online blogs when I visit a new place is very helpful for parking and access details. When I go to other places, I hire guides because I don't have the access, knowledge, or time to figure it all out. Additionally, I like to support local guides to areas I visit; my experience is that most are excellent, well worth the investment, and boost my success rates considerably. Wherever you fish, be safe, legal, and responsible.

We all know and love our home turf best in every way. We live there, where our friends and the fish roam and we know where they are. Because of this, I have the advantage when fishing with people who don't live here; they often beg me to "let them catch a few." I study the beach sandbars, holes, and rocky ledges, looking for places where stripers lie in wait or travel through for their tidal dining favorites. Once I know those spots, I can rely on them like clockwork, barring major weather changes. It's home-field advantage, and the odds are in my favor.

CHAPTER SIX
GOOD BONES

Fly fishing for bonefish is an exercise in self-deprecation and masochism and is completely degrading—until the lights go up and all the pieces come together. I am not an expert on catching bonefish, but I *am* an expert on everything one can do wrong while trying to catch a bonefish. Some people close to me have said I am like "a dog with a bone," lovingly of course. I hope my sharing the many things that can go wrong will lead you to success. Hang in there, go fish, and keep trying is my best advice if you really want to enjoy bonefishing, or bone-hunting as it should be called.

Bonefish have a wide range of distribution from the Central and South Pacific, including Hawaii, Florida, the Bahamas, the Gulf of Mexico, Antilles, and throughout the Caribbean down to Brazil, as well as some West African waters and parts of the Indian Ocean. I have only fished for them in the Caribbean, Belize, and off the Florida Keys. They are notoriously easy to spook and just as hard to see. They're often called "gray ghosts" due to their silver sides and darker black or olive backs. They are masters of disguise, thus the nickname. I think of them as more a silver cruiser than anything, since most fish I see are cruising along, smoothly and almost invisible, until they spook. These elusive characters can literally come on and off a flat and swim right past you without you even being aware of their presence. You could have an armada of bonefish coming at you and never know it until they make your position and screw so fast you're scratching your head thinking, "Well shoot, I didn't see those fish."

I began bonefishing in Eleuthera in the Bahamas after Karen and I started what would become annual two-week tropical trips to escape the Maine winter. I wasn't excited for these trips at first, until I discovered bonefishing. Now I love them! I love the break from the cold, and I absolutely love the fishing. All my mistakes have made me a decent "gray ghost" stalker. I do it in board shorts, a fishing shirt to protect me from the sun, ball cap, and light tackle pack. Being a minimalist keeps it simple and I've honed my skill enough to have with me just what I need to do the job.

Eleuthera is known for having some decent do-it-yourself bonefishing, with access to attractive flats and relatively low fishing pressure, or at least it did. On one visit, Karen and I skulked around the island getting lost down many dirt trails leading to the flats and even located some fish. Testing our rental jeep was arduous as we maneuvered over sizable boulders and along wet roads to reach the shoreline in remote portions of the island. I landed a small bonefish at the location of our beachfront cottage on Russell Island, but my success was both a shock and an accident. I hadn't seen that fish and was simply blind casting into deeper water, like I do when striper fishing, the only way I had ever saltwater fished. I would learn there are much better ways to go about the business of finding fish. I think it was pure luck I landed that small, sixteen-inch bonefish.

I had been told to fish the flat by the gazebo on the incoming tide so out I went. After several hours on the flat and as the tide overwhelmed it, I was dejected and noticed a person several hundred yards away. Every few minutes I'd see his arms go up high with his rod pointing to the sky. He was fighting fish! I had to see what he was doing and worked my way in his direction. Fortunately, he was working toward me—so I knew we'd intersect courses.

Normally, I would give space and not work toward another angler, but desperate times call for desperate measures and I didn't have a clue. When he got closer, I waved a friendly, sort of "will you help me" kind of thing and played a damsel in distress. He smiled and came to me, obviously happy to help. I explained I was a northern salty and this was all new so could he please share a few tips with me? Well, I hit the jackpot. Jared and I chatted until we spotted a half dozen fish coming at us; of course he saw them first. He coached me to get low, lower, even lower . . . only one or two back casts, then drop the fly five to eight feet ahead of them. Let it sink and wait. When he said to strip, I did, and the lead fish grabbed my fly and, of course, like a good northerner, I set that hook hard. Right! Broke off. Jared was kind and patient. We didn't see any more fish and the tide was fully in, but I loved that fish for taking my fly. I was down to about three useful flies, having broken off several on bonefish, barracuda, and the bottom. He gave me about ten of his flies because he was heading home the next day. What a gift that nice man was. God will reward him with many beautiful fish in this life, I hope.

In the beginning I viewed the sport as an endless list of the many things that can go wrong. Now I know the problem was partially me—muscle memory, a striper-wired brain, and impatience. I learned the hard way—doing it all wrong, over and over again, until I finally got it right and experienced all the necessary details of proper bonefishing—the sighting, low profile, fly placement and presentation, hook, fight, landing, and release.

Bonefish aren't called the "gray ghost" for nothing. They blend perfectly into crystal-clear water with a white sand background. If you're lucky, you might see a shadow bouncing off the bottom or the dark back when the fish is swimming right at you. I have been unknowingly looking directly in the eye of a bonefish until it was so close it could have picked my nose before racing to the far lagoon—"Geez, I didn't know there was a fish there!" I have at times felt that sense of not being alone, yet I could not see a fish. Suddenly, one will magically appear. Or not. It happens. We miss seeing fish in time and we miss ever getting that shot. Guides are often paid to be the eyes for us when we fish, even if we know how to fish successfully. Like sea legs, each time it can take me a few hours or a day to get my eyes trained to see the invisible racer. I have been with guides early in my tropical fishing career while they were barking orders of fish telling me the bearing and range and I couldn't see a darn thing. You can blindly throw where they say to, but it sure helps to see the fish yourself and make a clean shot. Also, your idea of "two o'clock, fifty feet" may vary from that of your guide. That's one reason I do a calibration drill of exactly what my guide sees as that reading until we agree. Still, I am *so* much more dangerous once I see those fish!

Trying to see a swimming fish is one thing, but what about once they have fled the premises? We know once we've spooked the great armada of bonefish because it's painfully obvious. A group of bonefish or even a single one that has been rooting on the bottom for bait will leave a puff or mud cloud when they spook. Hundreds or thousands of fish having had a feeding frenzy will leave a flat looking like the muddy Mississippi. I have learned from guides to try a few casts in the muddied area as a few fish may still be hanging around, but generally, they will all have left the party.

Then there's tailing fish. Bonefish will stick their snouts in the bottom to dig up bait while their dorsal fin and tail stick out of the water, twinkling and winking in the sunlight. My eyes have played mean tricks on me where I swear I see a tail, but suddenly it disappears, only to reappear in the same or a different location. I swear they seem to know when you look in their direction and can turn "invisible." Sticking even a perfect imitation in front of a tailing bonefish can lead them to tackle your fly or completely ignore it. Why? Who knows? They're bonefish.

In February 2018, I went to Deadman's Cay, Long Island, Bahamas on a weeklong bonefishing guided excursion with seven other anglers. It was my classroom for learning how to see, entice, hook, fight, land, and release good bonefish. In the course of those six days I caught around thirty-five bonefish, but the last day was the culmination of all I had learned.

Jerry, my guide, was the size of a linebacker, probably twice my weight and a sweetheart of a guy. We laughed and told each other some of our life stuff. In the middle of a sentence, while we leaned against each other's sweaty shoulders and both stared into the shiny glimmering water, he whispered emphatically "Sue, two o'clock, eighty feet—big bone." I could sense that meant this was important, but couldn't see the fish.

"Get lower, shhhhh," he said, and we were both on our knees in the water. "Lower," he commanded, so we crouched lower. I thought, "If I get any lower, I'll be on my belly."

"Okay, one o'clock, sixty feet, can you see him?" Finally, I saw the dark shadow of the bonefish in front of us, now closer to twelve o'clock and heading directly at us, constant bearing, decreasing range, like a torpedo.

"Can you hit him?" said my linebacker guide. I was trembling too much to speak *and* cast, so I just took the shot, knowing exactly where to place the fly. Heck, I had been doing this for five days now and had a clue. We were both holding our breath, and I could feel his huge shoulder against mine, the sweat pouring down both of our faces. Or were they tears? I'm not sure. I had placed my small shrimp imitation about five feet ahead of the bonefish's last known position and waited, until the usual command of "strip, strip, strip, wait . . ." which I was doing on cue, and properly now on my own. When the fish inhaled my fly, I waited just long enough before strip setting, then raised my rod high once he was on the run, and we were off to the races, the reel screeching bloody murder!

Once a bonefish is hooked, barring obstacles like mangroves to tangle in, they make several runs separated by short rest periods and, unless you get spooled, most fish are landed. This one turned and headed for the next zip code and my rod was up as high as my five-foot, three-inch frame could reach. I held on for dear life. Within seconds I was well into my backing and fretting about losing it all as I started running, dragging my linebacker behind me, yelling, "We gotta go with him or I'm screwed!" We were quite a sight sprinting after that fish (as best as I could run in a foot of water with a fresh gash in one heel still packed with sand and the steri-strips falling off). Finally, the fish stopped for his first breather and I regained half of my backing. A saltwater reel usually has 200 to 250 yards of thirty-pound braid backing under the fly line as insurance and I needed it. Repeating similar moves three more times, we chased and gained more and more back onto the spool until getting that fish to hand. I urged Jerry to stay with me as I feared I needed him for the landing, which was still not in sight. I made the mistake of letting my knuckles get whacked by the unwinding reel handle and swore unrepeatable words out loud while Jerry searched for his breath. My heart pounded in my chest and I spooned cool eighty-degree water to my head between sprints.

Finally, I was winning the battle. I rarely worry about losing fish, but fears of this one breaking off or taking my entire line remained firmly in my brain for much of the fight. The fish was getting more tired than I as we prepared to handle it, get a quick picture, and safely release the gem. Jerry estimated it around eight pounds. A very nice fish. I was giddy with delight despite the pain of my bruised knuckles. We took a few cell phone pictures and revived the fish, while searching for any nearby sharks before releasing the biggest bonefish I had ever seen. My coach, guide, and linebacker friend hugged me like a bear and said "Nice job, Sue!" I cried a salty tear.

Before I go hunting for bonefish, I do a bit of homework. I learn as much as I can about a particular place and read about where to go, the best tides, moon phase, and productive flies for the area. Being on a dormant flat that doesn't hold the bait—and thus bonefish don't come—is just a waste of time. I generally fish the low-end of the incoming tide on a nice flat and stay long enough to see them coming in after bait. Early morning and early evening can be very good, but the right tide, even in the middle of the day, can bring fish, if only I can see them! Aimlessly casting when I haven't seen a fish only tires me out and scares away what I have not yet seen, so I wait until I see them before making a cast. Save the arm. As I said, I have learned a lot of lessons about bonefishing, I will break out a few in the following paragraphs.

Lesson: Watch the Weather

As hard as it is to see bonefish on a clear day, they are extra difficult to see when it's cloudy. A mix of sun and clouds is at least better, and when the sun peeks out, it can be like someone flipped a switch and suddenly you realize that you are surrounded by bonefish. Weather conditions on the salt flats can go sideways in a heartbeat. Walloping wind and cloud cover sabotage and hinder performance and tip the scales toward the fish in a New York minute. If I have booked a guide and then see it is forecast to be mainly overcast, I will consider checking if the guide can move my scheduled day. I really try not to bail out as they have planned on me for the day.

I once found a nice flat at Long Key State Park in Florida where bonefish can be big, although they've become harder to locate without a guide. With the tide coming in, I rested on an old tire that was still dry on the flat, waiting for the tide to reach me. I slugged my water bottle, ate a hard-boiled egg, and patiently waited, thinking, "That power bar in my pack sounds good too, but I better pay attention and save it for later."

The next thing I knew I was surrounded by six inches of water. And I realized I had two big bonefish ten feet directly behind my tire. They had to be ten or twelve pounders, but the water, and our memory, does magnify things. What could I do? Moving meant game over, so I blindly flicked a short cast over my shoulder and slowly twisted to see how I had done. The fly was perfectly placed in front of the pair. However, they watched my fly pass right by their noses with no interest whatsoever, then swam off. Amazingly enough, I never did spook them. Lesson learned. Sometimes it's best to let the fish come to you rather than moving in search of them, especially if you cannot see a thing under overcast skies. Just don't fall asleep or meditate too hard or the world will pass you by—ahem, that is to say, the bonefish will just coast right by.

I try to know where the sun will be when I am on a flat and approach it so I can have the sun behind or at least quartering me. If I cannot see into a blazing glare, I may as well not be there because the fish see me long before I see them, and that isn't a fair game; they always have the home-field advantage.

Polarized sunglasses are a must, and a cap with a brim to cut glare helps a ton. Bonefish have beautiful big eyes for a reason and no other fish compares to them when it comes to sight, speed, and smell. Sometimes I will even search from dry beach, not even getting in the water to avoid the problem of them seeing or feeling me first. I may try from "skinny" or shallow water, casting to a deeper channel, although they have been known to travel into water just a few inches deep for food.

Wind is a factor as well, but I can usually deal with that unless it is blowing a gale. I have rarely fished in the tropics when the wind is blowing less than fifteen knots. The Christmas winds or trade winds kick in right around the holidays and it's just part of the game. Being able to cast in wind, even up to twenty-five knots is a great skill, which means good line management, false casting, and double hauling. Doing all of it is key, along with a low profile, minimal body movement, and minor water disruption, over and over again, with rock solid nerves while being dehydrated and sunburned. Sounds fun, doesn't it?

Lesson: Casting

Another lesson I have learned is to study a flat before trooping through it. This helps to maximize your environmental factors, cover the ground you want with the tide in mind, and keep other anglers a reasonable distance away. If someone is out there, identify which direction they are working so you don't go stomping through their route disrupting any fish in the area.

On a bonefish flat, it's vital to move extremely slowly while hunting. Some say you should drag your feet to kick up any rays and spook sharks in the area, but that also stirs up mud. The mud dissipates downcurrent and clues the fish that something is up. Then they vanish. I think it took me three years to truly slow down my wading speed to a pace that is quiet enough to let me see fish before they see me. I'm now Casper the Friendly Ghost.

Mastering the false cast to get the most of each one is key to minimizing how many casts you need to place your fly where you're aiming. Guides are superb at sighting and telling you where the fish are and where to cast, but it's up to you—the rod's in your hand—to make a great cast. You can't splat the water on each forward false cast; if you do, you will spook the fish. It also takes much-needed energy out of the cast. Nice high rod stops on the forward and back casts keep the line higher, avoid fly splats and form tight, efficient loops. Wait until the fish is close enough for you to place the fly three to five feet, or even more, ahead, depending on how fast it is swimming. Bonefish rarely stay in one place, so you have to think like them and anticipate their next move. The fly hitting the water at his nose will surely send him to the next zip code and leave you sobbing and alone. Last, but not least, false casts are tiring and will cut your day short from all that repetitive motion, which can possibly lead to injury. False cast as much as needed to hit the target and wait until the fish is close enough for your casting skill.

There is a diverse school of thought on where to place the fly for an approaching bonefish, which are always in motion. If the water is calm, you may need a small fly with little weight to avoid excessive splat, which will spook the fish. How deep is the water? Does your fly need to sink a bit before Mr. Big's arrival? Is your heart racing and can you get the cast off in time with accuracy? You wouldn't be the first to freak out when a few hundred fish are coming at you. Once you hit the lead fish, the rest are gone! Start casting early to ensure the fly is on location when they arrive because you may only get *one* shot. Make sure your slack line is clear when you hook up, and not caught on a buckle, boat clip, nippers, sunglasses, etc. There are so many decisions to make. I have put flies too far ahead and been caught in the grass and hung up when the big one gets to it. I have knocked bones on the head with the fly, completely pissing off my guide. I have waited too long, miscalculated the wind and put it in the fish's wake—and they don't generally turn back for it. As many informed guides, instructors, and chefs preach, presentation is everything!
OK, now you've made a fabulous cast and quiet landing. You're stripping perfectly and the fish inhales the fly. Holy mackerel!

You feel the bump and set like you did up north for every striper or trout you've caught in your life—and it works for them, but not for Mr. Bone. Your guide screams "Don't trout set on the f-in' bones!" My experience and the reason for the loss of many bonefish is that I set too early. My twitchy, fishy, gotta-get-this-right brain goes into *fire* mode and I set like a trooper, which often serves me well in northern latitudes.

Not so here. A guide on North Caicos taught me years ago that bonefish often just gum the thing for a bit, so if you set at the first touch you miss them. But waiting until I feel they have it and they have turned to run has resulted in more fish hooked for me. Patience is hard, but also don't wait too long to set because that gives the fish time to figure out he doesn't like shrimp that come with hooks and spit it out like a bad clam.

Bonefish can be little guys of just a pound or two, or double-digit linebackers. Either way, if you set like it's a tarpon yanking on that line hand with all your might, you may either pull the fly away before he's hooked or break off the eight-to-twelve-pound test leader. Both result in heartbreak and are errors I have made more than once. My little body is strong and I get excited over the hit, so I can set them harder than is needed. A nice moderate strip set straight back with the line hand usually does the trick. Then, and only then, after the hook is set, comes the rod tip issue.

Because I grew up striper fishing, I learned a certain style. With stripers, you feel a fish hit and set the hook with the big rod by hauling back hard, tip up and keeping the line tight. With bones, if you do that, you pull the hook away from them every time. They are turning with that fly and the strip set ensures a deep hook set in their hard mouths. It is then followed by raising the rod tip high while the fish takes his first sprint for the hills. Keeping the rod high clears the line of possible snags like mangroves or rocks and keeps a good angle to hold that hook in place.

Like all fishing, a tight line is always a good idea. Now my habit up north is a combination of the strip and rod set, which hooks fish every time!

Lesson: Line Control

Once a bonefish sprints for a while, you sure do hope your line isn't wrapped up in all the wrong places. Things I have seen or been hung on include: the deck hardware on a boat, gear left out, sandal or shoe clips, my legs, my guide's legs, other people onboard, motors, power poles, sunglasses, other rods, and gear hanging off your shirt. You name it! Lines have a way of finding anything and everything hanging out. I stow gear, remove my shoes, clip my toenails, keep nippers in a pocket, etc. Once that line catches while your fish is exercising his swimming muscles, you are done for. Tears are the result, done.

Be careful not to just let the running line go or all that slack becomes an avenue out for the fish as well, losing your hook on the run. When the fish takes a breather, retrieve as much line as you can because if you're not into your backing yet, you likely will be soon and need every inch you can buy back. Do it fast because they rest only a short period before the next sprint, and there *will* be another. See ya!

So, how to handle a run? Try to be prepared! My eight-pound bonefish took me into my backing on the first run and I knew I was screwed. Running with the fish in a foot of water isn't easy and tripping and falling on your face is a real possibility. I left Jerry, my guide at Deadman's Cay, in the mud. I had a fish in Anegada go into the mangroves, so my guide and I jumped off the boat and threaded my line and rod through several mangroves underwater, keeping that fish on the line to be landed. So, be ready to get in the water if you really want that fish; keeping booties on your feet is safe and wise just in case you jump in from a boat. I was still on fairly new replaced hips, but was faster than my less-fit guide when the adrenaline rush kicked in.

If you have never hooked into a bonefish, freaking out when the first one takes your fly and heads for the hills is not uncommon. It can be an exhilarating and frantic few moments as you realize you are *on* and your fish is *off* to the races! With every bone in my body shaking, my nerves frayed from trying for a very long time to get it all right, I recall saying to myself, "Don't freak, you got this," and I did. Once you've hit, missed, and landed a few, it becomes second nature to get it all right and land most of your takes.

Generally, you need to get that line on the spool and cannot plan to strip the fish in by hand unless it's quite small. If he runs again, the reel handle spinning in reverse at top speed can break a knuckle and if you have the running line in hand it can burn through fingers. Attempting to "palm" a screeching spool can result in burning as well so have the drag where you need it and be ready to make adjustments.

From knuckle-whacking reel handles to line burns to getting stripped, it all hurts when it happens to you and salt in the wound hurts worse. I have been a crying Sally too many times.

Lesson: Aftermath

Once you've landed a few bonefish, you know that if you do all of the above correctly there is still no guarantee of landing that fish. There is a happy medium between horsing a fish in too quickly and tiring it out so much that recovery is unlikely. Learning this safe place is important to the conservation of this wonderful species. The first run is probably the hardest, but they can repeat that performance several times before allowing themselves to be brought to hand. Sometimes one last thrash and jog attempt can occur close at hand but mostly they're wiped out by then. I think the most exciting part is the actual take and subsequent initial sprint. The best part, emotionally, is handling that fish in the water and watching her swim gently and safely away from you.

These are sensitive creatures. Imagine sprinting your bloody head off for two hundred yards and then getting a few seconds to rest before realizing you must go again or die! They're pooped when they get to your hands so keep the fish in the water and remove that hook, but revive the fish before just releasing. Just like humans cannot breathe underwater, fish can't do so out of it. A build-up of lactic acid and pure exhaustion will usually keep it from swimming for a few minutes. Nearby predators like barracuda and sharks may lie in wait, having picked up the scent. Releasing too early is something I have seen, but not done to my fish. I once watched a guy release a bonefish quickly, not ensuring it was revived first. A nearby shark came out of nowhere and attacked it, leaving a bloody cloud in the crystal clear water. That was hard to watch. I love pictures of my accomplishments, but only take the time if you see the fish appears to be recovering and in accordance with safe fish handling practices. You should keep the fish wet the entire time, only lifting it briefly for the picture, if at all.

Finally, I carry all that I need on the flat to fish, eat, and drink. A spare reel, flies, plenty of water, and compact food like protein bars are easy to pack and gobble in little time when calories and hydration are needed with little fishing time wasted. A small backpack keeps it on my body behind me where buckles will not hang up the line. I cannot put things down once I am out a mile on a flat so I simply swing the pack to my front to retrieve what I need.

Bonefishing has become my favorite angling activity due to its tropical setting and hunting nature. Jared, and many others since him, taught me the things that have helped me to now catch bonefish every time I get out in the tropics. I see them. I am stealth. I pick the right tides, places, and guides; or sometimes I go alone. I cast in various conditions, with the right fly, in the right place, with good timing and presentation, get the hit, set the hook, raise the rod on time, and hang on for dear life for each run. After the satisfaction of the fish eating my fly, running, and fighting are like no other fish in the sea, I finally catch and release the beautiful, sensitive, and amazing creatures unharmed. I do it over and over again, never growing tired of the game and always wishing for more.

Chapter Seven
Fishing Therapy

If you are anything like me, that is, you want to be fishing any time you're not working or otherwise committed, what do you do with extra time on your hands in a worldwide public health emergency like COVID-19? What's something we can do a rod length apart (generally eight or nine feet), without touching or breathing all over one another, is good for our health, gets us outside, and is fun by nature? *Go Fish!* It feeds the heart, soul, mind, and body.

I fished so much during the pandemic that my casting shoulder was actually sore and injured from the many long days I couldn't resist going. In March 2020, Karen and I had returned from the Florida Keys just five days before things started to shut down in Maine. For the next year I would fish several times a week with little other work to do. A few trout can be picked up during the slow, cold, uncomfortable winter months, even if you can't feel your hands and feet. Water temperatures in the forties make it painfully slow with dredging nymphs the only real productive way to hope for a hit. I wanted to be at full capacity when Opening Day arrived and was fishing sluggishly, at best, with an arm that throbbed ninety percent of the time. Ice fishing with a teeny jigging rod in my left hand was a good alternative, but that's not really the same, right? The days passed and I could fish somewhere, in a moving river open year-round, or on the ice any day of the week.

As a part-time safety consultant, I have some control over my schedule and can sometimes even plan my work around tides, weather, availability of others, water levels, etc. If the tide is right in the morning and I have a choice without putting off my client, I admittedly will select the afternoon for the work. I don't see any harm in that and have always taken pride in putting my customers first, followed closely by the fish. It's the only way I can make a living as a self-employed individual and have done it this way for nearly two decades.

In late February 2020, I was in the Carolinas for work. COVID cases were on the rise overseas and it was just starting to become a problem in parts of America. My colleague, a savvy safety professional, took the action to order one thousand N95 masks for his crews, a very proactive move it turns out. Karen and I had plans to meet in the Florida Keys for her spring break, a week of intensely planned play, which included fishing. I was fly fishing for tarpon and jacks and enjoying the warmth, like we do every March for a week. The pandemic wasn't "real" yet, but by the time we hit the tarmac to return home on March 6, it was brewing full throttle.

I worked into Wednesday that first week in March when COVID emerged as a real threat and things really started to be cancelled. That was the beginning of over a year-long isolation period and what morphed into little-to-no work for many, including myself. Social distancing (six feet apart), hand-washing, and facial coverings quickly became the norm, while some complied and others ignored warnings. Vaccines weren't available yet. Most of us, if fortunate to have not gotten sick, knew someone who had contracted it and been ill or possibly been lost to the virus. Karen lost her ninety-nine-year-old grandmother while in a nursing home, passing away alone only a week after her diagnosis. It was sad, frustrating, and taxing on all of us, and it continues. I fish. And I fish … and I fish some more. Work trickled in at an all-too-slow pace.

Throughout 2020 and 2021, fishing kept me and many other avid anglers sane. Classes continued at L.L. Bean and all precautions were taken, including canceling all indoor portions and offering them outside. I taught about half as many classes as my normal season and missed it terribly. But I fished. The usual April 1 opening day was moved up into March due to an early ice-out and a sympathetic State of Maine Inland Fisheries and Wildlife commissioner who wanted to support people getting outside to do healthy things in the crisis. Many fished by meeting friends on site rather than driving together, wearing buffs, a preferred clothing item anglers enjoy as primary protection from wind, rain, sun, and cold that doubled as perfect facial coverings. Some jumped in boats attempting a safe distance, while many just didn't guide or fish together in boats, hesitant to be in each other's breathing zones. It's crazy how the world has changed. But we fished.

I was out fishing on the streams as soon as the season was open, with time on my hands to try many new places I had never fished before. I was generally meeting one person, sometimes two, at the fishing location, gearing up a rod length apart and chatting as we prepared ourselves for the day. It was all pretty normal until novice friends needed help landing fish or fixing rigging, but we also dealt with that safely, stretching our buffs up to our noses and mouths to keep safe. Most places I can fish in freshwater and are worth getting to are at least an hour drive for me here on the coast. I could make up for that by saltwater fishing in my backyard all summer, only traveling down forty stairs until I'm standing in our boat or out on the tidewater. Driving together was not advised during the pandemic before vaccinations, so we met on the road and followed one another or convened on location. I can say I probably fished with twenty different people that first season, in twenty different locations, freshwater and saltwater. I am not normally out with other people quite that often.

Solo angling is still my favorite, not because I'm antisocial, but more because I move about regularly on a river and enjoy just hopping from place to place. Maybe it's selfishly knowing I am moving up or downstream without going around much, because I pick fairly remote places where I see few others, or I can go during the week while others are now at home, school, or working. I found myself discovering and hiking miles of stretches on rivers I didn't know existed, one to two hours away and feeling like I owned them. One such river I'll coin the River M. It was my nemesis, my joy, my playground, and my classroom for much of the pandemic year. Brookies and browns, large and small, live there. I experienced the joy of victory and the agony of defeat on the River M, which I began to view as Maniacal and at times Miserable. In April, I planned to hike the mile down river before fishing, where it was storied in blogs to be more productive and teeming with larger fish. It was still chilly in April, so I decided to stay in hiking boots rather than donning waders. This allowed me to cover more ground safely and scout as much as possible and , mostly, stay warm. I couldn't resist the first half-mile stretch of smaller pockets, although the online chats warned against them, and I had three brook and brown trout landed before hitting the first bend. "Not bad for the lousy part of the river," I uttered to myself and continued. It did not produce down river as I'd expected so I returned to the upper stretches, yielding three more fish, six total, and three miles of hiking wasn't a bad day, on the slow part of the River M.

So many trips repeated the above scenario in the next few months, some in hikers, some in waders, some alone and some with a friend or two. But the real story is the nice fish that materialized. Twenty-inch brookies and browns wet my hands as I contemplated a bigger net. A large boulder in the middle of one section became what I coined Alice's Condo, where I landed her little sister, a very nice eighteen-inch brookie, but Alice proceeded to ignore, then take, then break off my 5x tippet. I shared the story of Alice with several competent friends who never saw her, but I know she was there, until the water levels sunk too low to fish it by mid-summer and Alice apparently moved out. They're my friends so I think they believe my story that the mega brookie I met and lost did once live there. I still look for her on the River M, now that levels are back up and a new season is upon us but I've not seen signs of her yet.

The summer of 2020 was filled with so many fishing friends who wanted to land a striper. I can only say that everyone who came caught one. It was my year to deliver on promises to take friends fishing as I finally found the time with work at a shortage. At least I put it to good use. We talked and fished a lot and landed a few, but mostly it was a nice chance to connect with friends.

We were blessed with some rain finally by the fall of 2020. After a long summer respite from the River M, I made my way over to scout it out and found conditions fishable so invited my friend, Patty, to join me in hunting for the very pretty fall brookies Maine is famous for. Eager to return to the many great lies I had discovered in the spring and ready to share each of them with my pal, off we went to meet on site, buffs on, distancing a rod length and both of us geared up to fish independently, but together. A guy near where we parked barked at us from two hundred feet away that we were "not to follow him" which we found laughable as I knew exactly how to fish the river, having been there twenty times since March. I mumbled under my breath "not on your life buddy," or something worse as we rolled our eyes and headed down river right while he and his companion stayed river left.

We fished the lower stretches of the river hard for several hours, covering a good mile and didn't have a touch when Patty cautiously inquired, "Maybe we should see where that guy was fishing." I knew the stretch he was in as we saw him earlier and really liked the spot, but we knew better than to crowd anyone, especially someone with his apparent attitude. As we approached and could see he and his buddy were no longer there, we eased our way into the tangential leg of the stream. I had landed ten fish in that stretch in the spring and expected action. We found excited, hungry trout ready to grab anything shiny and gold like the bugger Patty was fishing with, so I begged her for one like it. A gracious and giving friend and angler, she handed over her next best imitation as we both proceeded to land three nice brookies inside of an hour. We even had a great setting for a short catch 'n release video ripe for posting on MWFF. The funniest part was my hooking an above average fish that scooted gingerly down-stream. My shoulder had gotten sore throughout the season so I was only armed with a fairly short, light, and soft five-weight rod. Having a bit of trouble turning the fish to me for landing and unable to follow it down this particular run, I handed Patty my rod as I tried to net the brute. Somewhere between her holding the line tight and me trying to reach the fish it became a long-distance release (the fish lost the hook). We never got a close look at it but it felt like a good sized brookie. It happens. That short side channel on the river was the savior of our day that we laughed about for some time.

Lesson learned: Always follow the guy that says, "Don't follow me!"

The saltwater scene saw countless tides holding fish and opportunities to share it with others. I boast that every person who came to my area to fish with me actually connected with a fish, either by having a hit or catching at least one. We fished in the sun, pouring rain, incoming and outgoing tides, high and low slack, times I never thought of as the best time to be fishing, and we caught fish. Friends who had never landed a striper on a fly did so. Others that had never caught anything at all did so—and we danced. I took their pictures and laughed, we screamed like school girls when they hooked up, and we posted on our fishy newsfeeds and group sites boasting about our successes.

———————

I grew up with a rod in my hand. I am extremely fortunate to have had the time to learn the fishing trends and techniques early in life. I now have a work schedule that often allows my indulgence, a partner that puts up with it all, and enough to make it happen. Yes, I'm lucky and I "live a rich life," as one of my dear friends often says. I'm blessed with so very much: family and friends who know I love it when they come fish with me. We talk, laugh, cry, and learn together; we fish and yes, we catch, and then we release them with wet, cold hands and hope for another. Life *is* good.

CHAPTER EIGHT

RAINBOWS IN THE WILD

One byproduct of the pandemic was the drive it gave many people to return to the outdoors. Although Karen and I are avid outdoorswomen, we spent even more time hiking, driving around the state of Maine, and yes, fishing. I fished with about twenty different people during the pandemic that I had not fished with before and caught more fish than ever. I had a sore shoulder to show for it.

In the middle of the pandemic, which made indoor activity risky business, Karen and I bought an Aliner pop-up camper. It was a relatively inexpensive rig with a sofa that pulls out to a bunk, a table that converts to a second full bunk, a sink with a counter, an A/C unit, a refrigerator, and storage. It's small, light, and easy to boondock with for simple trips. To boondock means to camp in the rough—no water, sewer, or power.

Our first trip was to Hastings campground in Gilead, Maine, in the White Mountain National Forest, only a half mile from the Wild River and a few miles from the Upper Androscoggin (or Andro for us locals). It wasn't a fishing trip per se, but we know I can turn anything into a fishing thing, so of course I studied and planned for where I might be able to sneak in a few casts (though to be honest, "a few casts" is usually several hours of fishing). The attraction to this area was its relative remoteness, its small, primitive campground, and its proximity to both rivers. My Maine fishing license was valid. We hadn't even heard of the Wild River, just ten minutes from the New Hampshire border and stocked with rainbow trout. I was game. We were happy with the plan. We made a reservation that cost a mere twenty dollars per night.

This maiden voyage would test our use and knowledge of the new rig. However, we hadn't planned on how cold it gets at night so close to the mountains, even in August. We packed bedding that was too light and spent most of the night shivering. Remember, we were boondocking and had no heater. Morning came early so we eagerly lit the camp stove to knock off the chill in the camper. On the positive side, Hastings was a sweet and very quiet little place where we felt like we were truly in the woods. We barely knew anyone else was there.

There are so many reasons I enjoy fishing, but a huge reason is that I really find serenity and can relocate my sanity at times. It's not a secret that I don't drink alcohol anymore—at all. Let's just say I drank my share in the first half of life. My last sip of the stuff came on August 6, 2003. My annual sober anniversary keeps fishing in the forefront and reminds me that life is best lived one day at a time, attempting to move on from yesterday, and not getting too concerned about what lies ahead. Daily gratitude lists, motivational readings, and regular contact with other fellow travelers feed my desire to keep living sober, even when the going gets tough, and it does.

Our first morning awakening in the camper was August 6. I always acknowledge the date with extra prayer and meditation, which I had planned to do on the river. I am often awake before Karen and eager to get outside, and this morning I quietly slipped out of our bunk, made coffee, and filled my thermos. I was quiet so she could get some added shut-eye. I have learned I can't be a "sleeping beauty" if I want to catch fish, especially in August. Getting out before the day warms up and swimmers splash in the river is vital. Plus, trout are cold-water dwellers.

My gear was already out for a late summer hike with Karen mid-morning. First, my plan was to wet wade in water sandals and board shorts, lightly loaded with a four-weight rod and my fishing vest. It was cooler out than I expected, but I was only ten miles from the White Mountains so I wasn't really surprised and knew it would warm fast. The half-mile morning walk to the river was brisk and still on the darker side at seven, but I had taken note of a bridge I would use to access an open beach area.

The wooden bridge crossed the river just above a nice pool I had already eyed on the way into the area, so I crossed and ambled down to the stream's edge, half-awake on my first cup of dark roast and happy to be on the water. On the second cast I was on to my first fish, a six-inch pretty little rainbow trout. "Oh," I pondered, "there are fish here." I had a few short strikes in the same hole before moving further down river into a run that had a nice deeper section on the opposite side along a rocky ledge. I moved through the one-hundred-foot stretch below this run and what happened next felt sort of miraculous.

Over the next two hours, with the rising sun warming the morning, I landed eight rainbows ranging from six to twelve inches, and all oh so beautiful. I caught them all on the same fly, a size ten Maple Syrup I had tied myself (and I am not a good fly tyer). My feet and legs were cold. The river, fed by the White-Mountain source just up the road, was running pretty heavily. I slipped off a rock trying to access a sweet spot in the pool, bashing my kneecap hard on a rock, but did not really notice until later in the day. For weeks to follow this bruised knee remained tender, reminding me of a special day I had on the Wild. I took selfies with my cell phone and returned each fish quickly, all the while thinking that I never expected this to happen. I never saw a soul until Karen arrived two hours into my fishing time.

It was my sober anniversary and I couldn't be happier with the unexpected gift I was receiving. Not that I was getting overly emotional about a few small rainbows, none bigger than a ruler, but the lack of expectation and knowledge of this very pretty little river was special. Maybe it was the precise focus I possessed on this day, fueled by my keen awareness of the gifts nature brings each day, if we only give it our full attention and find our hearts grateful for the mere fact of being here to enjoy it. I'm sure this all came into play, and maybe those little rainbows knew I was harmless and would return them promptly to see another day.

Karen made her way down after a while and was elated to hear news of my success. At this point the fishing had slowed and I was chilled, wet, and tired so we returned to the camper for some breakfast. By late morning we hiked to that hole by the bridge and saw several children swimming right where those rainbows had been hitting, and I thought, "Hey, they're spooking my bows!" I giggled at the change of scenery from the early morning secret moments I had experienced only two hours earlier. We hiked through the area, discussing how these things just don't happen every day and may not ever again. The rest of the day was plain fun, hiking, sunning on riverside rocks, drinking favorite teas and coffee, snacking, and laughing. I fished a few places but never saw any sign of a fish.

The next morning, I awoke even earlier, and again slipped quietly out of the camper and ambled down to the same swimming hole across the bridge and along the beach—my special section of the Wild. Of course, I was keen to repeat the previous day's performance but there wasn't a fish to be had despite working the very same spot under similar conditions. Actually, it was colder and I was severely under-dressed even though I wore two fleece tops over my t-shirt. Shorts turned out to be way too light in what seemed below fifty degrees out and not much more in the water. The same Maple Syrup remained on my rod, re-tied just to renew its strength, my lucky fly. All the while, my mind kept returning to the day before, August 6, my eighteenth year sober anniversary and how fortunate I was to be there. I didn't see any fish, but it was still a beautiful day. Gratefulness filled me as I sat on a rock, cold, with a black and blue knee to remind me, sipping my dark roast as the Serenity Prayer rang in my head:

> God grant me the serenity
> to accept the things I cannot change.
> Courage to change the things I can
> and wisdom to know the difference.

This prayer helps me to remember what's important, and those little rainbows were a gift from whatever higher power is out there that gives me so very much.

We stayed out there for three days, fished parts of the upper Andro on our way back and never saw a fish other than those eight special rainbow trout on the sixth. We traveled north and south along the Wild River, stopping to walk, swim, and fish along many sections. I returned to the area the next November, and it was closed to fishing but I took a walk by that bridge, beach, and stretch of river, recalling our visit and those sweet little "bows." I'm so grateful for rainbows.

Chapter Nine

Marsh Madness

From 1987 to 1989, I served on active duty in Lake Charles, Louisiana. After that two-year tour of duty, I was sent back to the area several times in response to major disasters and was in command of a cadre of senior officers, the Emergency Preparedness Liaison Officers (EPLO), from 2008-2011, in a reserve billet. We were the primary point of contact from other agencies and organizations working with the Coast Guard on domestic emergencies, which usually ended up being hurricane responses, but did include the 9/11 attacks on the Twin Towers in New York and the BP oil spill in the Gulf. It was hard duty with regular responses, unknown timeframes, and short-to-no-notice recalls. Watches were long and could last for weeks or months with few days off. When we did capture a day of liberty, fishing was an obvious source of recreation and stress relief for many of us. Coasties are water hogs, working and living near or on the water and often taking up a passion for fishing, boating, and other water-related activities.

The coastal marshes of Louisiana cover about eleven thousand square miles and comprise some forty percent of the nation's coastal salt marshes. Wetlands, including submerged grass beds, coastal mangroves, floating marsh, swamp, and scrub are prominent. This is the largest contiguous wetland system in the lower forty-eight states. The Mississippi Delta, the confluence of the Mississippi River with the Gulf of Mexico, is a three-million-acre area of land and water that stretches from Vermillion Bay on the west to the Chandeleur Islands in the east. It is the seventh largest river delta on Earth and is the nation's largest drainage basin, running off over forty percent of the contiguous United States into the Gulf of Mexico. It's big and they don't call it the Mighty or Muddy Mississippi for nothing. It can be as thick and murky as chocolate milk, but notwithstanding storms, the waters clear up quite quickly in the Gulf.

Fishing is pretty darn good much of the year with high points for various species at different times. Wind, rain, and cold fronts affect the fishing, as I've learned the hard way! Don't think because you're in the deep south it is always warm. Guides know the waters, the fishing, and ways to get around that make most of our heads spin, even if we know how to navigate. They fly from one marshland to the next, zipping at top speeds through grassy channels, while sports like myself pray we hired the right one (most are very good).

My twin sister, Sandy, started her family outside of New Orleans and has lived there ever since. She is now a grandmother, so I remain somewhat tethered to the area, visiting every few years, and always include at least one day fishing. During my Coast Guard career, I was assigned to New Orleans and spent some serious time fishing for redfish (red drum or spot tails) and speckled trout (spotted sea trout) whenever I was mobilized for hurricanes or other emergencies. While there for six weeks after the BP oil spill, I spent my $72 per diem on fishing guides for the weekends, taking different crew members out with me to share in the fun and thank them for their six day per week, twelve-hour shifts; it was a small token of appreciation for the grueling schedule. Reds and specks are the best eating fish on the planet, so I packed some up for Sandy and her family as I could. I was serving it up in my New Orleans suite most evenings. I'm certain the housekeepers weren't happy with the smell of my flat, but I tipped them well to leave me to it, also begging for more dark roast. I am a neat and tidy cook so the mess wasn't so bad, but the smell of fried fish was inescapable down the entire hallway of the wing I was holed up in.

Fast forward to the wedding of Naomi, Sandy's oldest daughter and my niece. I was heading down for several days together and I tacked on a bit more time to visit with Lurilla, a Coast Guard Academy classmate and a dear friend. She'd been begging me for some time to go fishing together so this was our opportunity.

I tracked down a guide who had nice reviews, but honestly it was his business name that caught my eye. It was late March in the middle of the Final Four college basketball tourney when we were visiting, a time often referred to as "March Madness." "Marsh Madness," the name of a Louisiana fishing guide business, seemed an omen I should roll the dice on because Lurilla and I had played basketball together at the Academy. Marty Authement was the owner and his website said "guided fishing . . . nestled in southeast Louisiana is Terrebonne Parish, which means 'the good earth' in French."

Duly forewarned he had one know-it-all and one novice along, Captain Marty was game to take us. Most guides know that when a sport claims to know how to fish, they usually aren't quite at the skill level they claim. I explained my honest evaluation of my ability as "experienced with more to learn" while Lurilla was green and knew it. We mostly wanted quality time together and to get her into any fish, so the decision was to tussle with some reds. Turns out Marty's first priority is safety, followed by fun, sick jokes, and yes, nice reds. It was perfect.

We enjoyed some visiting time and got underway early
to meet Marty an hour from Lurilla's home in Thibodaux,
Louisiana. Marty was an outright Cajun gentleman who spent
winters in the south and summers north in Montana guiding
trout fishing. We knew right away it would be a treat.

The day started a bit slow. I put Lurilla on the bow for most
of the initial shots, wanting mostly to see her have the best of
them and really enjoy herself. Generally, when two anglers are on
a small boat one takes the shot while the other waits. We were
sight fishing, that is, waiting until a fish is spotted before casting.
I was fly fishing and she was learning to use a spinning rod. The
last thing you want is to have fifty feet of running line out on a
cast prospecting for fish that you haven't seen and the bull redfish
of your dreams comes gallivanting by ten feet away. By the time
you strip the line in and recast, that dream is a distant memory.
So we hold the fly in the line hand with a bunch of line stripped
and ready on deck or in a stripping bucket and stand at attention
awaiting the sighting and the highly trusted guide's command to
cast. The guide usually spots fish first with their well-trained eye
and barks out the position with clock designation (for example,
three o'clock is ninety degrees directly off to your right) and the
approximate number of feet away. Now I have learned that we all
understand twelve, three, six and nine o'clock well enough to hit
the general area; but the concept of distance varies from person to
person. I go over it before fishing starts to be well-calibrated with
my guide. Marty laughed as we did that but later we were both
glad we had.

Lurilla was learning to cast the spinning rod and getting
better with each lob. She wouldn't mind me saying her first few
looked pretty funny. Captain Marty and I exchanged winks
as we watched. On the first sight of a fish, she hooked into
a decent redfish and fought for a while before the line went
limp. I think we three screamed the same unrepeatable swear

Louisiana guide Marty Authement. A Cajun gentleman who coined "the drug is in the tug."

word simultaneously. I actually have a short video that shows Marty biting his tongue almost to the point of bleeding. Then we laughed and soldiered on. She landed a nice fish after that, and one or two more while I was thrilled to see my friend enjoy success. In her sweet southern drawl (which never really left her even after decades away from her Louisiana upbringing), she said, "Sue, I can sure see why y'all love this sport!"

The weather warmed up, jerseys were shed, jokes became nastier, and the day was drawing closer to an end. Four o'clock looming and I had landed only a few small fish on the fly. Out of the blue, Marty boomed "pair 'o hogs on the far bank, two o'clock, eighty feet. Sue, can you hit 'em?" Well, I can cast pretty well and my accuracy isn't too shabby, but eighty feet isn't easy for anyone unless the conditions are just right. And the wind was off my right quarter, the worst for trying to get that much line out such a distance.

I confessed, "No, not happening, let's see if we can get closer." He handed me a spinning rod, "How about with this?" I didn't say a word. Before those two hogs ever suspected, I shot a bullet directly at them, clobbering one of the bull twins off the shoulder; while its mate shot off in one direction and the dumb one that ate my plastic booked it in the other. We were on, the spinning reel screeched with that sound only an angler recognizes as music to their ears, while I held on for dear life. Lurilla is a calmer Southern gal but when she gets excited you know it, so the usual "holy s—, Sue, that's a nice one" was the only thing I recall. Marty was firing off the motor, preparing to make chase. Redfish fight like stripers to me, but their pull just feels more muscular. They aren't sprinters like bonefish and they don't jump per se, but do break water and struggle right to the finish. I could feel the weight of this being bigger than any I had previously caught. I logged a forty-seven pound striper as a teen and this wasn't that, but it was nice. Maybe twenty pounds, but all anglers embellish a bit on the size of fish they catch, right? We landed it sweetly, released it, and headed to homeport full speed ahead. Mission accomplished.

Lurilla and I thoroughly enjoyed fishing with Marty and highly recommend him to guide anyone in Montana or Louisiana, or wherever he may be. His mantra, "the drug is in the tug," with a long southern accent is cute, funny, and so true. We fish in hopes of, at the very least, enjoying the time outside on a river, stream, marsh, or bay. We secretly do hope for a tug and yes, landing the big one. As some say, it's not about winning, it's about playing. I wholeheartedly agree. Fishing is about time with loved ones or quiet time alone and shouldn't be about what we catch and how big they are. To be honest, any day fishing is enhanced by also catching fish and when someone catches a nice one, we all celebrate. Lurilla and I reunited after years apart, and we shared something we both enjoyed and will truly not forget. Catching a few nice bull reds together definitely helped and we have the pictures to prove it!

Four years after that fishing adventure, I returned to Louisiana for the wedding of Sandy's youngest daughter. I had to find Marty for a day while I was in the area. Fall can be an exciting time for red fishing. There he was doing the same thing in winter months and we made the agreement to fish the day before the wedding, the only one we could both swing during my short four-day visit.

We met in the same place out of Houma on a cold day for Cajun country, a sunny and brisk thirty-five degree morning. I had an L.L. Bean down coat as a gift for my sister and ended up throwing that over three layers (I had never planned on donning all at once) and off we went. The gift coat would end up needing a full wash when I was done sliming it with redfish. Even for this Mainer, thirty or so degrees at nine o'clock is cold in the Mississippi Delta while zipping due south to hit the marshes

Me with a magnificent redfish in Louisiana.

along the Gulf coastline. We were both cold and hoped this front had not pushed them out. The morning started slow and, although we saw reds, they were intent on ignoring my offering. Marty had warned that could happen early with the low temperatures, but that with the rising sun and warmth, prospects should improve. I was annoyed but hopeful as we were seeing fish, so I trusted my guide and kept faith.

This time I explained to Marty that I wanted to strictly fly fish and hopefully land a decent redfish. I would not resort to the spinning rod to complete my day, though there is nothing wrong with that. After I landed a few small fish, the familiar heavier and harder hit and tug came my way and we were on. Marty and I were together on the bow while he manned the trolling motor with a remote device in hand. The fish ran directly under the boat on his side and tangled the line in his legs, in the kicker, then in the stern on the main motor. My fifty feet of running line was half on deck as the fish was in close and Marty managed to get that wrapped in his legs, too. We looked like Laurel and Hardy, trying to get out of a pickle right quick, laughing and swearing at ourselves for being a couple of pros all screwed up, but we managed to clear the three snagged areas, all the while the fish was still on the line. That became my biggest redfish on a fly, maybe seventeen pounds. I then caught another, bigger fish that seemed to have a deformity of its spine like neither of us had ever seen. It was kind of freakish looking and didn't fight very well. Once again, Marsh Madness and my friend, Marty, came through with another chapter of memories that I'd tuck into my fishing files for a lifetime.

So, let me tell you more about Sandy. We were twins and we looked exactly alike when younger—so alike that only Mom could tell us apart. Dad guessed at times. We were close and spent most of our time together mimicking each other's every move. As we got older, we developed our separate personalities, but we remain a lot alike. As kids we often fished together, helping each other and keeping close company in the dark, on long beach walks, and with our friends. We'd soothe one another's fears, encourage each other, and share everything from food to fishing gear and clothes. We talked, laughed, cried, and covered mile upon mile walking, running, and fishing the beaches of outer Cape Cod.

We could write our own book just about the many things we did together or games we played with and on others. If one of us wasn't prepared for a test in school, we traded classes at times. Unfortunately, teachers are smart people (I know, my parents and brother all taught school), and we got caught pretty quickly.

We played basketball and softball together in high school and shared many friends. My favorite thing was sitting behind Sandy, if they sat us alphabetically, because *Sa* came before *Su*. We shared pocket notes and chit-chat as best we could get away with it.

Sandy was a witty, charming soul, and remains so today. Her wicked middle-aged sense of humor surpasses mine and is a joy to visit. My parents still describe her as a sweet and funny child, which I recall clearly. She only told little white lies about how she was catching more fish than the rest of us, something she shared with me in secret because we share *everything* (except boys today). When we were around five we used to chase each other around the camper at the beach. My parents had visitors now and then who noted how fast their child was, not knowing there were two out there. We ripped round and round the rig with boundless energy, laughing and screeching until we fell in exhaustion when finally she caught me and we were observed in the same spot. To this day I love that memory and how funny it was to my parents who knew our game and watched as unsuspecting guests peered in amazement. I love Sandy with a piece of my heart that just cannot go anywhere but to her and everyone knows it.

In 2010, I was drilling in New Orleans for the Coast Guard reserves. Sandy and I are both addicted to fishing, so we hired a guide to take us out on Lake Pontchartrain. This big lake can make you feel like you're on the ocean if the wind and wave action is up. It is a brackish estuary in southeastern Louisiana, with 630 square miles of pure fishing territory. An average of twelve to fourteen feet deep, it's oval in shape and forty miles east to west, twenty-four north to south. Sandy lives just a few miles from it, not far from the north shore. There are just scores of fish that can be caught in this awesome lake, including speckled trout, redfish, flounder, sheepshead, black drum, crevalle jack, and tripletail.

If I remember right, we got underway out of Slidell, Louisiana, in Captain Mike's small boat. Sandy and I were primed for what we expected to be a wild day. A kind, unsuspecting soul, poor Mike had no idea what he was in for. It started slow until we found our groove, picking up a few small reds and

Captain Mike had no idea what he was in for when he agreed to guide Sandy and me on Lake Pontchartrain.

specks. Within an hour we both started hooking fish regularly while the cursing, laughing, and screaming grew louder with each fish. We grew up in an environment where cursing when excited was the norm, as long as not among those offended. Add in a few years in the military and we thought nothing of the slang coming off our sweet lips. Any dropped fish was a "no good S.O.B." I'll just not say anything further; you get it. I put Sandy on the bow, the preferred position when two anglers and a driver are on a small boat fishing. She would hook one, then I would, and poor Mike insisted on trying to keep up with hook removal while we said, "We don't need your freakin' help, man!" That's actually quite funny to look back on, since we *did* hire the man. I imagine at first he wasn't sure what to think of us, and I'm sure our potty mouths put him off, but he quickly caught on that we weren't amateurs and really probably didn't need his help. I think he cracked open a beer and became more of a casual observer.

By noon we were a half hour from our Slidell homeport, several miles out along the North Causeway bridge, when Mike pointed out the cooler was topped off with fish and we were nearly out of bait (live shrimp), so we'd better call it a day. Mortified at that notion, Sandy and I simultaneously (twins do that) yelled "We're not f-ing done here, Cap, we're just getting started!" Mike looked green, but we were not throwing in the towel. So off we went, bow pointed east. I am absolutely certain poor Mike wanted to jump his ass overboard before facing the afternoon if what he had seen was us just getting warmed up.

At the dock he dumped our fish into another cooler, reloaded shrimp, and looked at us with what appeared to be fear in his eyes as he said, "I've never seen girls fish like you two." I think I saw a tear in his eye, but my sympathies were short-lived. We were pay-ing him well for the entire day and that's what we had in mind.

There is no point in belaboring the obvious, that we did more of the same all afternoon and by the time we hit the dock at day's end, were beyond giggling with joy, recalling each catch, and poor Mike looked just ragged. He still had to filet those fish and bag 'em up because we were filling Sandy's winter freezer. I had the biggest redfish, but Sandy had landed a big sheepshead (apparently known for their eating quality), and several nice speckled trout. She vacuum-sealed the filets in packs fitting for her family meal plans, I took some with me, and FedEx shipped a bunch up to our parents in Massachusetts. The greatest gift of that day was spending it with the one I split the egg with, doing something we both grew up enjoying together, and the pictures, stories and memories remain precious today. My parents shake their heads with tears in their eyes when we recount that day, knowing they gave us that priceless gift of life, love, laughter, and fishing.

It was just a riot, a day I hope to never forget and will likely embellish for the rest of my days. The sizes and numbers of fish landed goes up each time the story is told and what becomes clear is that we were in heaven sharing our common passion for fishing. Poor Mike, not so much. I think we paid him four hundred dollars for the day, and he worked so hard Sandy miscalculated the tip and gave him another two hundred dollars, which turned out to be best with what we put the poor guy through. We all slept well that night.

I'm guessing Captain Mike has marked his files to avoid taking us on his boat again: "These two are *double trouble*."

CHAPTER TEN
MAINE SLEIGH RIDE

I love fishing from my kayak although it is challenging
with a fly rod. I admit resorting to a baitcaster or spinning rod
when the wind is blowing, weeds are rolling in, or just because it's
easier in the kayak. The long flimsy fly rod is begging to be broken when a fish takes you under the boat or down to the bottom
in some of the holes I hang out in, and I need the backbone of
a stiffer rod to raise a brute to the surface. When being dragged
into the channel with a passing lobster boat or a tipsy tourist at
the wheel, it's a lot easier to get out of there if you've got a fish on
a rod you can spike and run.

Kayaks are speed bumps to Maine lobster boats, or so the
joke goes. I would rather not test that theory and I always wear
my brightest kayaking top, personal flotation device, and a bright
hat so they at least see me before running me down. Waving
a paddle overhead with a boat roaring at you full speed ahead,
constant bearing, decreasing range, is just plain scary. Actually,
the wakes of passing boats that don't slow down enough for us
smaller ones are the biggest concern as the wake can flip a kayak
easily, especially if the kayaker is on to a big fish. Despite the

challenges of fishing from a kayak, benefits far outweigh risks. I can access fishing spots I could otherwise not reach, and get exercise I wouldn't otherwise get, not to mention see many birds, seals, and other wildlife.

With a kayak, I can get into narrow, rocky waters without fear of running aground. I can beach my boat and stand in places I would never otherwise reach. I don't have to worry about the tide running out on me in action, leaving me high and dry. A motorboat caught dry on a dropping tide leaves you fishing and napping for six hours, until the rising tide. I haven't done that quite yet, but came close; one of my favorite hot spots is best on the high drop and I risked our boat grounding a few times attempting to fish. By the time I turned to see the boat's status, its bow was pointing to the clouds and I had to use a spare oar as a lever to push it off. Not good.

I fish from my kayak between May and October in Maine more than from our sixty horsepower, seventeen-foot motorboat we keep at our dock. I just can catch more fish from it. Maybe it's because I spook fewer fish using only a paddle, or maybe it's about being on the water's surface, closer to the fish, or maybe it's just simply being able to sneak into shallow water.

When I discovered pedal-driven kayaks, I was recovering from major shoulder surgery and looking for legwork I could do while my arm was in a sling. Although fishing in that condition was out of the question, I did buy the pedal-driven kayak. I had a long-term plan—my arms would be free to cast and fight fish, and I would be able to back pedal out of a rip or hole and resume a better position between casts. The plan worked. I have caught a multitude of fish and been able to exercise my legs simultaneously. I can back pedal easily to escape danger or simply to better tighten a line onto a fish. The only deterrent is my brain keeping it together enough to reel *forward* while pedaling *backward*,

I discovered pedal kayaks after shoulder surgery.

which is kinda like rubbing your belly and tapping your head at the same time.

One day I hooked a really nice striper in a favorite honey hole near what you might call the channel here in Harpswell, if there is one in this small, semi-protected sound. The lobster and pleasure boats stay pretty much *in* the middle of the narrows, away from any hazards and I stay *out* of the middle in my kayak for obvious reasons—you know, the speed bump thing. I was on to this fish mid-morning on a bright, sunny day and was wearing my usual bright gear while driving *Slayer*, which is what I named my pedal kayak. The fish was dragging me to the middle of the channel in what we call a Maine Sleigh Ride. That's when I started to hear the distant, familiar sound of a lobster boat's diesel engine. I looked left, nothing, then right and here comes *Easy Money*, one of the local lobster boats I know. He is a very good and considerate boat driver and has never been an issue for me, but he has to see me first, so I took no chances. I started to crank down on my baitcaster drag, having faith in the thirty-pound dacron I had it loaded with, while a light state of worry settled in. Do I cut and run, fight the fish, pray *Easy Money* sees me and slows, giving way, or jam the rod between my legs and backpedal out of the channel? It was a nice fish, but I mostly wanted to live. I am so darn glad Karen wasn't present to see this one.

It took ten minutes for *Easy Money* to get closer and by now I was in a dangerous position waving my emergency paddle. I had elected to roll the dice and was back-pedaling slowly while dragging this nice bass on the line, moving only a bit out of the channel with each passing minute. The linesider pulled harder than I and I wasn't making much way on him, but my butt was getting out of the way. The captain of *Easy Money* fortunately saw me, as he has many times over the years, and promptly reduced speed with a wave. He watched with his arms crossed as I landed a decent, maybe twenty-eight-inch striper in the middle of the channel. Navigation rules require a motorboat to give way to a kayak but, just like a pedestrian has the right of way, that doesn't mean we should just start waltzing across a busy street. I have bought lobster from *Easy Money*, waving him down to offer five bucks per, while he tossed them in my stern hatch. I promised to drop a twenty dollar bill on his boat the next trip out, packed neatly in a plastic zip bag taped to his console, with my business card inside. That's how we roll in Harpswell and it works. I'm glad he doesn't view my kayak as a speed bump and slows down readily. His lobstah is sweet, too!

One morning, I was sipping my dark roast on the deck and saw the birds working in the sound just off our dock. It was early and I was barely awake but knew I couldn't ignore what I saw—birds hitting the water, and fish breaking. They weren't pogies. Karen knows not to ask any questions and just shakes her head knowing on a summer day with me moving this fast that something is fishy. I left the coffee to chill, grabbed my personal flotation device, hat, sunglasses, ready bag with a few spare lures and my baitcaster. I prefer the baitcaster in the kayak because the reel is over the rod, which avoids the knuckle whacking that a spinning reel causes due to its location under the rod handle. The baitcaster also rests my right arm from overuse in fly fishing because I hold the baitcaster with the left hand.

My ready kayak was alongside the dock, which sits on the flats at low tide, but is afloat by mid-tide and ready to get under-way in short order, bow pointed to sea. I strapped my rod under the bow bungie, untied, and shoved off on a full high slack tide. Only about two hundred feet offshore the school of incoming fish was still feeding while the birds continued slamming the bait. The kayak is perfect because zipping up to a scene like this in a full throttle motorboat sends the bait and fish down deep and the birds scatter. With its low and quiet approach, paddling or pedaling, a kayak leaves them doing their thing, so I can approach and cast from outside the school of fish without sending them under. I was *on* immediately and subsequently landed ten schoo-lies in a half hour, all small and perfectly pure fun. The coffee was cold when I got back, but well worth waiting for. A quick thirty-minute fishing trip was all the energy boost I needed.

The biggest and best kayak fish I ever caught was only a few years after Karen and I moved to Harpswell. A favorite waterfront seafood shack was about four miles down the sound, making a perfect kayak ride on a calm day. I never got underway without my rod. Karen had a cold and wasn't quite herself, but had a hankering for their haddock sandwich, so we went for it. Just before reaching our lunch destination, I was significantly ahead of her and knew she wasn't well since she's normally a stronger paddler. I pulled in along a ledge I have since named "Monster Alley," because of the fish I landed that day. First cast, I thought I was hung on the bottom as my rod doubled over and wouldn't budge. Rocks don't pull back so I quickly determined that the bottom was moving and yanking me into the sound. This was no schoolie. I have no idea how I ever landed this fish, but slowly I got him to the surface while Karen got closer and I began yelling for help because I was afraid I'd flip the boat, never a good thing in cold ocean water. I also knew she had her digital camera onboard (we didn't have cell phones with cameras then). After several rod transfers from port to starboard and back again, I got the fish alongside my boat, struggled to remove the hook, and with one fell swoop was able to bring it across my lap for a quick measure with my tape. It was forty-two inches, and that was with a bend in its body! Its black eyes were the size of a fifty-cent piece. It was the second biggest striper I had ever caught.

I have trolled a rubber shad behind me in the kayak while paddling and caught stripers. I once had a striper inhale my shad into its mouth and out its gill to then be taken by another bass. I have countless pictures and memories of stripers ranging from ten to forty-two inches in my kayak. I now have a tape measure sticker along the right side of the kayak for quick checks. Because I release them all, I don't need to know their size other than for accuracy in the volunteer logging program with the state of Maine. Anyone fishing in Maine can participate in the Volunteer Angler Logbook program with the Maine Department of Marine Resources (DMR). Reporting of catches, locations, sizes and methods helps them to accurately track what is happening with the striper population for targeting of conservation efforts. There is also a Tackle-Buster Club for certain larger fish to be recorded and recognized.

The sleigh ride can be exhilarating and scary, and it isn't easy to land a big striped bass in the ocean on a small kayak that bounces around like a cork in the water. Add in the effect wind, current, and wakes can have on such a craft and things can get mighty dicey at times. Fish can be unpredictable, especially when they get closer to the boat and decide one last time they'd rather not be caught. The big ones run you deep and try to rub the lure, fly, or line off on rocks or anything they can find. Safety, as always, is paramount. I make sure my direction of travel is known, my cell is charged, and I am wearing something bright, including a personal flotation device. I have spare fishing gear with me, sometimes even a second rod. If I bring a friend, I put them in the heavier, more stable boat and stay close abeam in case they need help, planning to pull up to assist if needed for their safety or if they hook a nice fish. I always have a whistle to make noise, and stay close to shore and far from any boat traffic.

Catching fish from shore or the dock is much safer.

Chapter Eleven
Trigger Happy

In late December of 2019, Karen and I escaped from
the Maine winter by taking a trip to Anegada, one of the British
Virgin Islands. It took me two full days there to figure out that
I was chasing triggerfish. Yup, I knew they were fish, but I just
didn't know what they looked like until I went back to our
beachfront cottage and googled them. There they were, right on
the beach where we were staying, doing the same tail dance I had
seen on the internet, but never in person. They were nibbling on
a bed of coral, just like they are known to do, but I didn't know
that at first. Then a few days into our ten-day stay, a stranger on
the island told me to go down at sunrise to where I already knew
they were. It was a location a half mile down Loblolly Beach
from our cottage. We seemed to own the entire stretch for miles.
I was happy to get up daily to what seemed like endless walking
opportunities. The sun was shining without a cloud in the sky.
The sand was toasty on my bare white feet and it seemed I had
been launched directly into heaven!

The trip to Anegada was arduous with a domestic flight from
Portland to Charlotte. We spent three hours waiting there in the
United Service Organizations (USO) lounge munching on snacks

and checking messages online. The anticipation of this new place, where there was also some prospect of locating bonefish and other tropical delights, was palpable for both of us. Finally, we boarded the flight from Charlotte to San Juan where we spent one night in a beachfront apartment to catch our breath before heading to the island of Tortola, the largest of the British Virgin Islands. There we boarded a ferry to Anegada. It was one of the more fortunate travel days I have been blessed with, where everything pretty much went off on time. Nice!

Triggerfish are a tropical and subtropical fish found in shallow, coastal habitats of oceans throughout the world. Most are about eight to twenty inches in length. They have an oval-shaped compressed body, with a large head terminating in a small, but strong-jawed mouth with teeth adapted for crushing shells and coral. The eyes are small, set far back from the mouth, at the top of the head. As a protection against predators, they have two dorsal spines: the first spine is locked in place by erection of the short second spine, and can be unlocked only by depressing the second or "trigger" spine, hence the family name triggerfish. They often live around reefs, banks, coral clusters, and the like and can be territorial and aggressive. To me, they are kind of ugly and pretty at the same time, and I hear they fight hard. Their thick flat body can turn and book it for the deep blue yonder in a New York minute, but I wouldn't know. I read all of this.

Because triggerfish hang in shallow water and fight hard, fly fishers are eager to seek them out. They feed on crustaceans, using their oversized incisors to root around in coral, scaring crabs and other inhabitants out of their homes to scarf them up. When they are not aggressively feeding, they are often antagonistically protecting their dens and they can attack a proper bait imitation with a vengeance. Casting has to be extremely accurate to get the fish's attention, and they are often observed tailing on shallow coral beds. Because they use those teeth to break up coral, they are challenged with hearing anything around them, including the splash of a presented fly. They can be surprisingly selective in taking a fly and difficult to bury the hook due to their small, toothy, bony mouths. They will also rub off a mono leader on the coral leaving the angler crying on the beach. A challenge any angler is happy to accept, if she even knows what's in front of her. This is *exactly* what I experienced on Loblolly Beach.

Loblolly Beach is located on the islands' northern shore and is known for very good shore-entry snorkeling and great visibility in the water. It has several miles of seclusion and unspoiled sand and coral. We spent ten days there walking the beach, snorkeling, and just hanging out reading, with an occasional drive to find a restaurant, latte, or a new place to explore.

Glorious would put it lightly until Karen picked up a nasty cold. She stayed in bed longer in the mornings. I found myself trekking solo to the beach at sunrise with an eight-weight rod in hand and basic gear (flies, nippers, leaders) in a small pack, sunglasses, sunscreen, and a good cover for the sun, in board shorts and a tee. I was off, hoping to catch anything that swims. On my first morning out, I saw tan tails, thicker in nature, maybe fins, sort of flipping around in the wash, some just a couple of feet off the beach in one-foot waves, lapping the exposed coral with an incoming tide. Others were further out on the coral bed, about fifty feet offshore where it was still shallow, maybe waist deep. I cast and cast and just couldn't get a take, getting hung up at times on the sharp coral. I was nearly clocking them off the head with my accuracy. I was barefoot, not realizing I'd soon want to venture into a coral-covered minefield, which could give foot and ankle scratches that cut right to the bone, creating a blood trail sharks love to sniff out.

Two hours after my first sighting of these fussy buggers, they disappeared and I was back to check on the patient. This went on for three days. The next day, while Karen slept, I put on protective booties and headed to triggerland, knowing they'd be there like clockwork. I had marked the exact spot on the coral bed with a long stick in the sand above the highwater mark. Fish do tend to return to the same places at the same time of the tide and day through their favorite cycles, i.e., two hours in at sunrise for a few days around daybreak. This time I waded into the warm eighty-two degree water on the close side of the reef and decided to work offshore, casting toward the ones nearest to me. The tide was coming in, so I knew I had to guard against getting stuck further out on the reef. Otherwise, I'd be swimming with my gear overhead, something that was neither safe nor wise, but the fishing brain can make bad decisions in the heat of battle. Again, nothing hit, although in retrospect I think I had a bump or two. I was using a shrimp pattern because there doesn't seem to be a fish in the sea that doesn't like shrimp. I landed the smallest permit, the size of a man's hand, the first and only one I have ever caught, but it jumped off the hook as I gently pulled the leader toward me, avoiding my handling it at all. I was disappointed not to get a picture, but with my location being waist high in water and coral I didn't have the extra hand to mess with my phone and keep the fish wet for a safe release. It did me a favor, and now likely still swims, older and fatter.

I was happy trying, or whatever I was doing, still not sure what I was seeing but knowing for sure they were not permit. Then something that spooked—a six-foot shark cruised toward me from eighty feet down the beach, ten feet offshore, in a foot of water. I was fifty feet out, up to my waist, with warm white water breaking over my shoulders. I knew I'd never get to the beach before Sharky was between me and dry sand. I was more ticked this shark was screwing up my trigger-happy morning than afraid it would attack me—a mild, but sincere distraction. Karen and I see and swim with nurse sharks often while snorkeling but, like most humans, I can be spooked when trapped in an area with a shark lurking. I had a cut above my bootie from a graze with the coral that I knew was seeping blood into the water because it stung. I had also noticed a red cloud near my leg. "Uh-oh," I muttered. The fear mounted.

I stayed put, making no commotion, and stopped casting. The shark eventually cruised past with no obvious concern for my being. I could only consider that I didn't know what kind of shark it was, and I had better get out of the water. I was too deep and at risk of getting caught on the reef with the incoming tide, despite being a good swimmer. It would be nice to get in safely with all of my gear not completely immersed in salt. The booties I had wisely donned came in very useful, decreasing scrambling time on the coral and minimizing cuts to my bony ankles and shins.

The next day Karen felt better so I dragged her down the beach to join in the fun. I don't think she found it as exciting to look for triggers, but she was mildly amused and curious about what I was after. A lifeguard wasn't the worst idea, but I feared mine wasn't going to let me in the water since I had shared the shark story (big mistake). It was a beautiful early morning, we were completely alone, with coffee-filled travel mugs in hand and my gear strapped over my shoulder. Morning exercise is always a welcome thing for us. I marked the big stick location and yes, they were there, as before, still not touching my offering. Karen kept shark watch while I tried to get the attention of any fish in sight, but there were no triggerfish.

Later that day we met a guy who told me to go down to that reef at sunrise or sunset on a rising tide, and that they were triggerfish. A shrimp fly was a wise choice. The shark was probably harmless, and he encouraged me to go for it. I knew all that by now, but it was nice to hear I wasn't crazy about the triggerfish or the shark! I tried every shrimp and crab pattern in my pack, never getting one to actually take my fly. I surmise now that they may have been nibbling and swatting at it, but the imitation just wasn't close enough to what they had in front of them. I didn't feel like a failure because they are known to be tough to catch and I really have no experience with them other than seeing some snorkeling. It's maddening to be on a flat all day, see fish—bonefish particularly, but triggerfish too—and not get one to strike, then go snorkeling and have hundreds swim right by you in ten feet of water, clear as day. Somehow, they know I'm not carrying a fly rod and the GoPro I may be holding is pretty useless for catching anything but pictures!

I went every day for the rest of our stay and never saw another fish out there. I hooked a few barracuda in front of our cottage, lost a few flies on those toothy buggers, and even saw a few triggers during daytime walks. I think the tide had gotten too late to fit the sunrise/sunset scenario and we would be gone before the tides would be right again. That was my one and only chance to catch triggerfish, and I didn't even know it most of the time! I will be on the lookout for them in the future and would love to catch one (and release it) on a fly.

CHAPTER TWELVE

WAIT FOR IT

During a good chunk of my time in the Coast Guard, I was often in the Gulf of Mexico. I was in the Coast Guard Reserves at the rank of commander and the senior emergency responder for domestic disasters or events, leading a group of Coast Guard officers called the Emergency Preparedness Liaison Officer (EPLO) program. I was often in the Gulf, because many of the events involved major weather events like hurricanes there. My duties involved organizing the dozen or so senior coast guard reserve officers nationwide to be ready to respond on short notice to any national event. We were the "tip of the spear," the primary point of contact reaching all levels of other organizations, as well as the funnel to Coast Guard resources. Basically, the EPLO was the person everyone else at a command post needed to find if they wanted Coast Guard assets to do something. It was important and meaningful work and how I spent much of my final ten years of my thirty-year career. When foreseeable events such as a hurricane loomed, we pre-deployed. Our deployments often involved long days, weeks, or even months of daily shifts. It was a tough duty that sometimes involved very serious threats to human lives and property. I stayed glued to the Weather Channel during hurricane season, so much so that I could anticipate when and where I'd be headed next. My go bag was at the door and I got quite good at booking myself anywhere on the shortest possible flight itineraries.

Sandy and her family, who lived outside of New Orleans, were often impacted by monster storms, so I had personal interest in the work as well. If anything was threatening them, I was doubly concerned. Fishing was often in the back of my mind, but mostly it just wasn't going to happen in those situations. However, a few trips did turn out to support my habit.

For example, the Florida Governor's Hurricane Conference was an annual event that I attended once to help me better prepare for my role leading the EPLOs. I think it was in May 2009 when I attended with Sam, a Coast Guard commander and colleague also involved from the active duty side of our New Orleans unit. Luckily, Sam was very interested in fishing also, kind of a newbie, I would later find out. We connected before the conference and made loose plans to try to fish together, but nothing was known yet of our class schedule or if there were any free days to break away. These things usually had very full agendas that left little room for play other than dinner and drinks for those who liked to spend their time that way. I wasn't keen on big dinners out or the drinking scene so some clean fun fishing was something I was always up for.

The first day of the conference went off without a hitch. I had located a guide online, Gavet Tuttle, and arranged for him to take us out tarpon fishing that night because our days were chock full and it was the only available time. Sam was one of the most easy-going guys I have ever met, let alone worked with, so he was game for anything. Tarpon like to eat at night and most of the guys (I was the only woman in the class) were headed out on the town. I was only a few years sober at the time so hanging around my hotel room wasn't attractive and I definitely had no interest in going out to party. It was an easy decision to hire a guide and go fishing. Additionally, Sam was game to split the tab so it was a no-brainer.

Sam and I sprinted to our respective hotel rooms upon release from class. A quick change of clothes, gear, and the plan was a "full day" of guided time from four to midnight, and we'd be tucked in just in time for seven hours of sleep before class the next day began at 0800 hours. Gavet thought we'd warm up with a few specks in the backcountry channel enroute to our destination near Miami Beach. I played with the fly rod and landed a few while Sam watched, not being a fly fisher. We both really wanted to wrestle with tarpon on any rod, anywhere, so we pushed our skipper to keep motoring toward the tarpon grounds, time being of the essence. We were well aware it would be a long, tiring night and would likely leave us whipped for the next day, but sober and tired was better than hungover and tired. He agreed.

It was getting dusky by the time we were offshore on the Atlantic side of the Florida coast, looking at the evening lights of South Beach, Miami. I'd never been there before and found it odd to be looking at city lights while fishing. It was an odd mix of beautiful ocean, blanketed by the urban backdrop of the city. I was elated to be fishing for monsters but taken aback by the setting. There seemed to be a channel of heavy running tide that Gavet was putting us on as we prepared lines with live shrimp on a single circle hook, no weights, no frills, and mid-sized spinning and conventional rods. Even the rods weren't as big as I would have expected for what could be two-hundred pound fish! It's hard to believe but tarpon are perfectly happy sipping or sucking down single shrimp as small as my finger with mouths like buckets. They will do that all night long, gobbling away with abandon like a moviegoer eating popcorn.

Our guide briefed us both on the rods and the fine art of trolling shrimp (basically run a bunch of line out and spike or hold the rod and stand by for heavy rolls), but I was tuned out as I knew how to use them. Sam, it turns out, wasn't familiar with the rods, reels, drags, hook-setting, and other intricacies of fishing that one learns in a lifetime of doing it. I was pumped and begging to get on with it. I elected to hold the rod, finding a spiked rod to be a complete bore, and wanting to feel a monster grab my baby shrimp. On our first drift through, and by then it was full dark, I felt my first ever tarpon strike and set back with all 120 pounds of me. I was on, but then I was off in less than two seconds. Gavet explained not to set right away, which he probably had covered in the pre-fishing brief that I had ignored, like I knew it all, ahem. His scholarly advice now was that you must wait upon feeling a fish on the line, a count of five, then haul back hard to set the hook. He stressed *hard* because tarpon have very hard mouths so driving that hook into it isn't as easy as with other species. On the next swing through it happened again, so I waited but that eternity of five seconds was much too long for my fish-wired brain, and I set probably at about three seconds, again missing the fish. Our captain laughed. Sam giggled with joy at our action, and I fumed at myself for missing again. That was it, third time's the charm and off we went for the third swing through the channel off Miami.

It is unmistakable when a tarpon grabs your shrimp and it's utterly impossible not to want to drive that hook in immediately, but, finally, I did wait for the full count. When the fish first gummed my shrimp I boasted aloud, "I have a fish on, boys." Gavet replied, "You know what to do, Sue," and Sam put his big joy-for-another-smile on quietly, as I counted aloud to be sure they knew I was on it, then whoa! I—set—the—freakin'—hook! The battle was on. Gavet grabbed me by the hips, a fairly intimate move, but, being a gentleman he explained, "Sorry, Sue, but I don't want to lose you overboard."

It was just a dream as he held me to the deck, offered a fighting belt while I swore and screeched, "I've got him!" and Gavet muttered, "I've got you." Forty-five minutes and several athletic jumps later, having refused the fish-fighting belt, we landed that monster alongside the boat. Gavet, with his tarpon-grabbing-gloved hand holding tight to his bucket jaw and me scooching in for the pic, and that memory was sealed in the best shot we could get without compromising the fish. Tarpon are majestic looking beauties. They have very large scales and are quite shiny and silver in color. Most notable, they have huge bucket-like mouths to gulp air, and they jump when hooked to gain maneuverability. We estimated the fish to be about my weight, 120 pounds soaking wet. I was on the moon. Although Sam was fishless, he was ecstatic to witness it all. I was literally vibrating with thoughts of "Oh my God, I just landed my first-ever tarpon!"

Gavet professed that the landing rate for most anglers is about sixty percent and that's what I did that night, landing three of the five fish that hit me. I never missed after that first one and the others were about fifty and seventy pounds. Sam never caught one. I checked his drag on the way in and found it nearly free-spooling. It was so loose I'm guessing he had hits and never knew it, poor guy. I think he was

Me and Gavet with my 120-pound tarpon.

truly happy watching my crazy fishy brain and body fight each
one. We laughed all the way back to our hotel, paid our guide
generously and high-fived good night, see ya in seven hours.

The next morning my elation continued as I awoke with
memories of the second shift on Gavet's boat, cruising off of
South Beach, and fighting tarpon. There was no brain fog, no
hangover like the ones I had back in the day when I was drinking,
and I was downright cocky when I arrived in class with the guys,
Sam by my side glowing with anticipation of the stories that
would inevitably surface. Our plan was hatched over morning
coffee but we'd let that wait for a while as our classmates wondered what we had been out doing half the night. We prepped
the instructor to slap our pictures up on the overhead projector
on cue as he asked the class what we had done to pass the evening
hours. Bleeding eyes, pounding heads and dry throats complained
they had too much to drink as they begged our leader to go easy
on them. Sam and I wriggled in our seats like school kids who
knew they had nailed the homework assignment and we waited,
a count of way more than five seconds. The instructor saved us
for last and looked at Sam, then me, but Sam wanted to be the
announcer, so I deferred. When the pictures went up we smiled
together like a married couple on a honeymoon and I think the
entire class moaned together, "Holy s—!"

Sammy and I were quite pleased with ourselves, alright. I
only wished he'd had a match with one of those silver kings like I
did. I did tell him to be sure to check that drag any time he goes
fishing, but didn't have the heart to say he probably had fish on
and off all night and never knew it.

Chapter Thirteen
The Big Three

Having grown up on the salt water and been totally immersed in striped bass fishing in my youth, I've naturally gravitated toward that, rather than fly fishing in freshwater. My skills at trout fishing have improved exponentially in recent years, but I still have a lot to learn. So to land three big brown trout in a ten-day period from the same river was a miracle. I do not know how I did this. Right place, right time, skill, luck? Some combination thereof? Regardless, it happened and I have a few friends who *believe* me. One friend was with me for the third one, which should have been her fish. She doesn't let me forget it.

The first brown was on December 11, 2020, on a Southern Maine river, a local haunt that I hit often during winter months because it is open year-round. I can fish it all winter unless the shelf ice sets up, making it unsafe. I made my way down just below a bridge where an enticing reverse eddy sets up by a deeper hole, although I had never had a touch there in several years of fishing it. An L.L. Bean buddy told me he catches fish there often. It looks fishy so I keep going back and hoping. I preach to all of my friends and fishing students to approach a stream low and slow because fish do have a cone of vision and can see us much of the time. I catch more fish dry in my hiking boots than I do wading because I'm not in the water spooking them, and I stay very low and proceed very slowly. I once watched a guy approach a run on Grand Lake Stream crawling military-style on his belly and he caught several fish where I had just been skunked. Even if they don't see us, they sense our presence and spook easily.

On my first drift through the eddy I stayed on the edge of the current, where the foam line is a dead giveaway to the sweet spot, and I settled in. I was rigged with a huge white wooly bugger and a small olive leech in tow on a tandem rig as my weapons of choice. I have secretly loved tandem rigs ever since my good friend Kate taught me to "Double your chances, Suze!" She is better than I am at fly fishing, so I usually follow her advice, not afraid to admit my openness to getting as good as she is. I think I was managing my line, but was mildly distracted and the rig had gotten sucked down into the current down-swell. I thought it was the bottom, until it started pulling directly across the stream and I knew I was on! My soft five-weight rod was out straight in seconds with line peeling off the reel. My heart was suddenly in high speed and my brain clicked on that I was onto something bigger than I'd ever had before. "Holy cow, wowza, oh-my-God," and a few expletives slipped off my lips out there, the only one on the river. Actually, these broodstock browns don't fight very hard when running, but they can be big, so it's the weight of the fish more than anything that one has to lug in, and against a good current I risked breaking off. I had a 1x leader on for the big wooly bugger, but 4x in tandem behind it was tied to the bend of the hook for about a foot, to a size ten olive leech. In ten minutes I had him at my feet, kept him wet in the net that he overfilled, and snapped a few self-timed selfies for posterity as I shook my head in disbelief, thinking, "I need a bigger net." It was a new experience to catch a trout so big his butt was hanging out the end of the net. I had read the stocking report and knew

eighteen of these twenty-inch broods had been placed in this river
a month or two before and I probably had one of them. They
could also be holdovers. *Ah*, those tandem rigs—it was the leech
he had engulfed!

The second big brown was late afternoon the day I fished
with Bri at the Mousam River in Kennebunk on December 12,
one day after I'd hooked, but lost a huge brookie, and visions of
that beautiful orange flank-flash before breaking off still haunted
me. I left that river and Bri by mid-afternoon and kept my
waders on, knowing I would stop at the same spot on the way
home, looking for some comeuppance. But it was after three and
the shortest days of winter were upon me, so I had little time. I
headed downriver in waders, testing each pocket big enough to
hold fish with no luck. I knew I was down to a half hour until
dark, the temperature was dropping fast, so the next big pocket
I approached low and slow, hoping this would be it. I still had
the huge white bugger on my line from the previous day, but had
changed to another soft hackle in tow, having lost the first one to
the long-gone morning lunker brookie. I replaced it with a similar
wet fly and prayed. My first cast to that last pocket was perfect
and settled into a little swirling motion, which quickly came tight
and held in place. Suddenly, a linebacker of a trout had me down
and under and wasn't budging, a move that sometimes feels like
a hang up of some sort, but then I saw his side as he turned away
and knew my luck had turned in an unbelievable way. An eternal
optimist regarding angling, I rarely think about losing fish once I
hook them, but after the morning's heartbreak, I confess that all
I could hear in my brain was "Don't lose this one, don't lose this
one." I didn't and big brown number two was landed just before
sunset. Again I thought, "I need to bring a stiffer rod and a *bigger*
net!" I was the only person on the river, cold and giddy with my
reversal of luck. I couldn't wait to text Bri a selfie and call her to

share in my elation. In her usual sweet and supportive way she celebrated my luck as if it was her own.

Big brown number three was also on a tandem rig, this time the big white bugger and a nymph in tow; he took the bugger. It was December 20 and my friend Patty was hot to trot for one of these bruisers, so I dragged her to the same big eddy up river as the first brown, just below the bridge. Afraid to be the one to catch any fish lurking there, I put her in my exact boot tracks where I had stood in the snow only a week before and told her where he had hit. I duly advised her to stay low and slow, which she grunted at. She is a prior student of mine and a very good fly fisher who has been working hard at improving her skills, so she didn't need me to guide her in any way. Yet it happens to all of us—she hung bottom after ten casts and was abruptly out of commission, so I gazed at her with my look of "guess I gotta do it." I made a cast from my spot twenty feet to her right, into the reverse eddy side of the hole, where she wasn't hung up. On the second drift through I was on. Again, I knew immediately it was a relative of the first two big ones, while Patty shook her head in disbelief. She's since confessed that she secretly wanted to toss me into the cold river. Although we love and support our friends and enjoy their success, when they do this sort of thing we all secretly ask ourselves, "Why didn't I catch that fish?"

Up above, from the street on the bridge, a woman and her husband watched and snapped pictures. The woman, Wendy, yelled down to ask if I was Sue, but I didn't recognize her at the time. She had been a fly fishing student of mine and promised to send me the pictures she took, having watched the entire scene.

The third brown was lighter in color, an inch shorter than the first two, but fatter. It didn't fit in my net either. There I was sporting three fish over twenty inches within ten days, in December, from the same river, possibly three of the eighteen broods stocked earlier in the fall, or holdovers from previous years. How does this happen is all I can ask, and is it luck or skill or knowledge of the river or all of the above that led me to this success? I certainly had more than my share.

I have always felt fishing is a mix of skill, knowledge of the area, tide, moon, weather, currents, flows, etc., possibly with some luck mixed in. Being in the right place at the right time, using the right fly or lure, presenting it in the right way all combine to make one successful or not. I do feel luck may have arrived for me in December 2020, the end of a very difficult year with the pandemic. My work had been cut back and much of the new spare time on my hands had been spent fishing, both fresh-water and saltwater. Despite the terrible circumstances, the time blessed me with better fishing than I had ever yet experienced in Maine and my freshwater skills improved significantly. I do think it is a direct result of time in the water, for one.

One lesson "the big three" taught me is that I need to carry a big enough net for the largest fish I may catch in any given area. Round upwards. Those browns all hung their bruisin' big butts out of the end. Just as the boys in *Jaws* needed a bigger boat, I needed a bigger net!

Chapter Fourteen

Oddities

The more I fish the more I know something funny, beautiful, odd, or unexpected seems to happen every single time I go fishing. It may just be that I'm keenly aware of my surroundings and don't miss a trick, but I swear, something happens on each excursion. I'll notice things like the loons that seem to hang off our dock or seals bopping around with the tide. I also see the horseshoe crabs in the gravel shallows searching for mates, something I notice each late spring right around when stripers arrive here on the midcoast. The horseshoe crab spawning season usually occurs during May and June when large numbers of horseshoe crabs move onto sandy beaches to mate and lay eggs. Their spawning habitat generally includes sandy beach areas within bays and coves that are protected from significant wave action. A small area I fish is perfect for them.

Karen isn't really into fishing, but now and then she picks up a rod and shows off her natural athletic prowess. She has the ability to pick up anything and do it well with little instruction or practice. I also think she brings me luck because often when she shows up on the shoreline, I get a hit or hook into a fish. "Here comes my good-luck charm," I often say.

We were fly fishing for trout many years ago in Nova Scotia and the evening hatches were significant in early summer. Karen wasn't that adept with a fly rod, but she could drop a fly twenty or thirty feet, and that was all that was needed. On her back cast, which was tapping the water behind her, she hooked a salmon parr. She actually may have hooked it on her forward cast and it was so small she flung it over her shoulder on the next back cast, then forward and back into the drink the little guy went. She still tells me how she wondered why I was catching fish and she was not. Her dry fly was getting repeated swats, but no takes. When she finally checked her hook it had broken off on the rocks. It was funny.

I have broken off hook points on my back cast where the embankment rises up on an angle behind me and unless I stop the rod very high it can hit the rocks back there. It has led me to check my fly often, especially if I'm getting hits, but not hooking the fish. Stripers are often voracious feeders and take flies readily. It's a good idea to check the fly frequently anyway to insure it's traveling correctly, doesn't have hackle up around its neck, and resharpen the hook.

At times if I am trying to paddle my kayak to a new location, I will let my jig drag behind the boat, inadvertently trolling, which is actually an effective way to fish. If there are a lot of weeds in the area it's a pain because you just cannot keep your line clear. On one occasion my rod started to bounce from its temporary anchor between my legs and was almost dragged out of the boat. I caught the rod as it began its bound over the gunwale. Lesson learned: if I'm going to troll in the kayak, secure the rod well and don't think a fish won't hit it. I landed that one, luckily. Another time we had stripers in the area and I had a hit, but the striper inhaled my lure and blew it out his gill, then another grabbed it so I had both on the line! Just odd. One hook, two fish. Kinda unexpected and not your everyday occurrence.

One spring I was fly fishing for trout on a river in Midcoast Maine. It was still chilly and I didn't know the river yet so I was fishing in my hiking boots, eager to cover the length of it—scouting and in need of exercise more than fishing. I find I often actually catch more fish in my dry boots rather than waders because I am able to roll cast more effectively, and I spook fewer fish by not getting into the water. Admittedly, if I hook a nice fish I may get wet landing it, and I have slipped into the drink a time or two in my boots. I landed six fish that day on a river I didn't know well. One of them was a fourteen-inch brown trout that I didn't actually catch. I hooked the line with a fly on it that the fish had eaten from someone else. It seemed a prior angler had hooked and broken off on this fish and the hook remained in its mouth with a few feet of line dangling from it. Odd.

I'm not interested in following a stocking truck. It seems the fish remain somewhat stunned and uninterested in eating right after they have been plunked into their new home, in this case, a local river. I had been on the river fly fishing for an hour without a touch and saw the truck come in and park on the other side of where I was. I took a break and observed, as they dropped hundreds of ten-inch trout into the chilly water about one hundred feet from my location. After they left, I got back in the water on my side and again didn't have a hit. Then I thought, "Well, those fish are hatchery fish and eating pellet-like morsels all day, every day, so put a small nymph on and dead drift through this eddy here." On the first drift through I was on, with my little eight-foot, three-weight rod, a tiger putting up a spunky little fight for me. I proceeded to hook and land about twenty small brookies in twenty casts, pure fun. I thought I'd give those little guys some exercise to get ready for real life in the river. I guess I was wrong about freshly stocked trout being uninterested.

On another day with Marty Authement guiding me for redfish in southern Louisiana, one of the fish I landed had sprinted under the boat and headed to the stern, catching line on the kicker motor at the bow and around the seventy-horsepower motor back aft; my guide wouldn't mind me mentioning it was caught between his legs and under my foot as well. It was a fiasco for a couple of pros and we roared "get off my line man, whoa, he's still on, holy s—!" God, we laughed until we cried and I landed that broad fifteen-pounder, my best redfish on a fly. Then I caught the oddest fish I have seen, an even bigger redfish with what appeared to be a curved spine, something neither of us had ever seen. It was kind of sad and ugly and weird. Of course, Marty said only I could do that but *he* guided me to it, so I blame him.

Karen and I went to Costa Rica in January 2009 to play tourist for a few weeks. It wasn't a fishing trip and I wasn't yet far enough into my fishing obsession to pack fly rods or even look for what I might chase while there, but I do recall contemplating it. Finally, a week into the trip, I gave in to my need to do something fishy and looked for a local guide. We were in the Puerto Viejo area, a small beachside town an hour from the Panamanian border, where there's no McDonald's (fine by me), and kids learn to surf as soon as they're able to walk. The place is rough around the edges, colorful, laid back, friendly, and nestled nicely on the tropical Caribbean coast. Its vibe isn't luxury resorts and golf clubs, which is why we chose it, and a fresh coconut on the beach under an almendron tree while reggae plays on a nearby loudspeaker is the norm. It's definitely quaint compared to San José and, from what I hear, the west coast of Costa Rica.

We stayed at a simple beach house, learned to surf with a local instructor (with washboard abs), and enjoyed warm tropical breezes and rains on a daily basis as we listened to howler monkeys and slowly studied the metabolism of the local sloths, trying to act more like them with each passing day. It was nice, but not without worries of local petty crime and nuisance problems. I was getting bored and was itchy to try some fishing. I finally found a local guide who would take me and let me use his gear, good thing because I was gearless. Expectations were low and I was pretty uninformed as to what to expect so I went with an open mind, just hoping to learn something new and get a tug or two.

We met the guide at a local beach, where he had about a twenty-four-foot heavy wooden open skiff rigged with a small motor. I think there were a few old spinning rods on the deck but I was focused on the boat while Karen was exceedingly glad to *not* be joining us. I don't remember his name but he was a charming man with a family that included a wife and several small children. Then out of the brush a young couple appeared, wanting to join us to fish so I shrugged and thought, "Why not, there's safety in numbers." We negotiated a price of three hundred dollars for the day, which they would cover two-thirds of and I decided I had little to lose, so we shoved off, leaving Karen waving and I'm sure thinking "better you than me honey!"

For lack of either wanting to, or actually not recalling details, it matters little—long story short, we didn't get a half mile offshore and the heavy rollers started, leaving David, the male of the loving couple, looking very green. He was an athletic, strong-looking dude. His girlfriend was my size, slight in stature. Within minutes he was tossing cookies over the side while his fiancé and I laughed and kept fishing, which was actually handlining. Neither of us had ever handlined before and the boat captain was pulling in fish after fish, so we gave it a go. I don't even recall what we were catching, but they were small ocean fish, which he was thrilled to keep for his family table. All of our fish were tossed on the deck for him to pack up later. By nine in the morning, David was begging us to go back ashore, and his fiancée was beginning to look green herself. She also was soon down for the count. Captain Ahab and I were still hand-over-hand lifting fish to the boat. It wasn't my cuppa tea, but he was content, or so it seemed. The happy couple were sick as dogs, now both begging to go in. Right around that point Ahab was lurching over the side by the motor (I'd thought his color was changing to one of greenish blue) and I was getting concerned for our safety. With not a life jacket to be seen (retired Coasties don't like to be part of *those* sea stories), a wicked sick boat captain, and two crew incapacitated, I finally gave in, feeling terrible for sharing the boat fee and watching them in misery. We pointed the bow for home and raced to shore where Mrs. Ahab awaited, looking like she was used to seeing this show and glad to have food for the week. We duly paid them and left while I swore that I would never ever again hire a boat without doing my homework.

Karen chuckled, likely thinking, "I saw that coming a mile away." I left an L.L. Bean spinning rod and reel as a tip because he didn't own any decent rods.

I teach fly fishing part-time at L.L. Bean in Freeport and have had so many funny experiences with students and coworkers (some that are best not written). One was a typical summer day when I had six students for a short ninety-minute class to learn basic fly casting. One customer was clearly suffering from having imbibed too heavily the night before, reeked of whiskey, and was a bit wobbly on his feet. He was a lovely man who really wanted to be there, but couldn't put it all together. I was patient and supportive as I stuck it out with him to teach the basic four-part cast. Several times he begged me to let him have a much-needed smoke as I explained it was a smoke-free area and I just couldn't let him do so. Somehow, while I was making rounds in the field with the other five students, my man disappeared, which left me mortified that I'd missed his exit. I studied the field and roadway back to our classroom area to no avail. Then it became clear: the outside porta-potty had outright smoke signals wafting heavily from the top roof vent! I chuckled. I decided to leave it untouched. I do tell the story at our annual training and we all laugh and relearn to *always* know where each customer is. Nobody got hurt, I wasn't reprimanded. When ya' gotta go, ya' gotta go, or as we say in the military "smoke 'em if ya' got 'em."

In another L.L. Bean class, I had a young couple among ten people in attendance. They were both sweet and pretty good anglers. When we hit the pond to try our hands at a few stocked rainbow trout, the guy was with me while she went to the other side of the pond. He hooked a notable fish and managed to get it landed without my help, but when he got it in hand he begged me to take his picture. I didn't carry my phone that day so had to use his, which was buried deep into his front pants pocket. Now I'm not an easily embarrassed person, but I was a tad shy at digging in this stranger's pockets with nine students watching intently, and a co-instructor and his darling wife laughing at the entire charade. He begged. I stuttered. He begged. I looked at the wife, who knew what he wanted, and she yelled "Do it!" I dove into the wrong pocket first, then the other, and managed to locate nothing but his phone and shot the picture. I don't think it phased him a bit, but I now carry my own cell phone.

I had time on my hands during the pandemic, so I dug out my old float tube to inspect it for viability. I've never been big on float tube fishing, but had tried it years ago on the saltwater sound where I live. It's a great workout with flippers on, kicking my butt off, but I never really found it the way to fish here. All kinds of hazards can become real with motorboats who may not see you, getting caught in current, cold water—you get it. It was a hot day in July 2020, and, although the ocean water barely gets into the sixties some summers, it is very refreshing when the summer heat comes, so I often swim or wade. The thought of the float-tube in my board shorts and bathing top was lovely on this particular day. Karen watched with a curious smirk I knew meant "what are you doing with that thing out there?" I proceeded to inflate it with my foot pump, did a full inspection to see that it was holding, grabbed my flippers, and then rigged my baitcaster with a four-inch plastic shad, something stripers hit readily here. Again, she shrugged and laughed off my usual obsessed-with-fishing behavior. I was wise enough to affix a thirty-foot piece of line to the tube in case I wanted to tie off or got into trouble and needed a tow in. After a half hour of heavy kicking against the incoming tide for a workout, it was time for a rest, so I tied off to our mooring about sixty feet directly in front of our dock. Karen was on the stand-up paddleboard nearby and likely keeping half an eye on me, still shaking her head I'm sure thinking she's not going to catch anything there.

The day was glorious. It wasn't about the fishing. The breeze was perfect, the water refreshing. A hot late July summer day in beautiful Maine. I was in heaven, not really focused on a fish, but I did notice it was the high slack tide, that magic ten minutes when the water is no longer incoming, but hasn't started out yet, when for some reason fish often like to hit, until they turn off again. I began to cast, but didn't expect even a sign of fish. On the second cast I was on and more surprised than anything. The baitcaster had a pretty deep bend in it and the tow-line was maxed out as I hung on in surprise. Landing a twenty-four-inch striper in a float tube is not easy with everything in motion, including me. My photographer, after shaking her head a few more times, took pictures from her paddleboard while I was in the tube.

An hour after that float-tube foray, a woman was attacked by a great white shark only miles away from our location off Bailey Island, and did not survive. It was the first fatality from a shark attack in two hundred years here, the second shark attack ever, and was a major headline for weeks. Attacks this far in the north-east are rare; they are hardly ever recorded in Maine at all and unheard of in Harpswell. We see seals. Apparently, people swimming in wetsuits resemble seals, which great whites like to eat. After this tragedy, Karen made it clear I would not be float-tube fishing again any time soon in the salt. Back in the basement it has gone to collect dust. It was a good try.

The oddities just keep happening. In July 2021, I was fishing with my friend, Patty, on a lake an hour north of home, where she rents a cabin for a week annually. I try to get there for a day so we can goof off in kayaks, fishing in the sun. For a couple of pretty savvy fly fishers, this really is a day to play and not take our fishing very seriously. Usually in bathing suits, we pack fly and spin rods now, knowing we will catch sunfish, crappie, and small and largemouth bass. We have learned, as you will soon see, that a net is a good idea. Actually, a *big* net is a better idea!

We push off from the camp dock, sometimes one of us falling in as it can be precarious, turning more and more serious as we approach the nearby cove where the best fish hang out. What began as a lighthearted panning for small fish, turned into memories of the intermittent surprises we've both experienced there. My first time there, I had a huge largemouth grab my wooly bugger, right before my eyes. I observed the entire attack, set on the behemoth, had him on, and dropped him boatside. I swore like a sailor. No more goofing off here. Patty, a sort of angelic being who never swears like I do, patiently cajoled my loss and ignored the terrible words that slipped off my lips. We seriously turned to the fishing. The fish was duly named Walter from the story *On Golden Pond*, a huge bass that escaped the old man and grandson, and was finally caught.

Later in 2022, I got a text from Patty while on a ferry to go fishing with some guys at Martha's Vineyard. It had a picture and a note that she'd caught Walter! I couldn't believe it as I shared in her joy and lamented that it was the one I had missed. Now the chances that it was the same fish are slim, but we sometimes like to think we're chasing or catching the one someone else missed. I am certain she enjoyed being the one to land him while I still cursed his escape from my hands. I was genuinely happy for her. It turns out hers was a big smallmouth bass.

Then came our most recent visit to the lake. She had two friends from out west visiting, and we abandoned them to the dock to soak worms while we frantically paddled over to the cove, the scene of earlier crimes. I dropped a smallie on the way, and a few small fish swatted at her fly. I had a very small spinning rod, again, goofing off while in the back of my mind I recalled "there are a few big fish here and you're screwed if you hook one on this thing." My legs went up on the side of the kayak as I splashed cold water over them to chill out. Then I had a loop down deep in my reel spool so I took a longer cast to get to it and a bit of a "bird's nest" developed. This took me at least five minutes to dig out, with no luck untangling, so I cut the line at the spool and began pulling the line and jig I was using in by hand about thirty feet.

There I was, pulling in slack, legs hanging out of the boat, the bird's nest secured for later trash, and the handlining in of the jig stopped abruptly on what I figured was bottom. I tugged. It tugged back. I tugged harder. It tugged harder and ran the other way! "Oh my freaking God, I'm on!" I yelled. She was too far away to care. I thought it was small at first . . . until the next run. I paid out line carefully by hand, simultaneously pulling my legs in and yelling, "this fish is big, I need help, bring the net!" She was one hundred feet from me, her approach at first was too slow for my liking, so I yelled more, "I have a big bass on this line in my hands, hurry!" I got the bucket-mouthed bass to my boatside, grabbed her net and in the first scoop got three-quarters of his body in it, with several inches of tail hanging out. We looked at each other and screamed, I don't even know what. And that was *my* Walter.

As I ponder why I fish and why it makes my life so rich, it must have to do with the element of searching for the next surprise of what wildlife I may see out there, who I may meet, what I can learn and, yes, what the fish will do. Any avid angler knows while we don't always catch a fish, we rarely regret going out. Karen often says, "how was casting practice dear?" when I come in with no stories of fish, and my reply remains "oh, it was nice out there," or "the loon is back," or "you won't believe what happened!" That's why I fish. I always feel renewed, even if dejected with a loss. The memories of those that got away stick in my head sometimes like a bad dream, but really are fond experiences that always beat most other things in life.

Chapter Fifteen
The Hard Water Jig

I loved ice fishing as a kid, got bored with it as an adult, then fell back in love with it in a completely different way. During the pandemic, boredom increased and work decreased. Netflix became the evening norm and could easily overtake daytime activity if I wasn't careful. Regardless, I'm like a puppy and don't sit well for very long unless I've had my daily dose of outside activity and exercise. That translated into a need to feed my fishing addiction.

I caught on to fly fishing for trout through the winters, and now I don't bother even stowing my gear; the time between thoughts of "it's too icy to go," and "it's early spring, I gotta get outta here" makes it just not worth the work. I'd bring an outfit in from the rod rack in the garage, one at a time, for seasonal maintenance (cleaning, lube, line checks, etc.), then put it back in place knowing I would be out again soon. I began to wonder why I was bothering.

During the pandemic, Karen and I escaped sickness of any kind, including colds and flu, because we barely had contact with others and, when we did, it was from the prescribed six feet away and with a mask. I got the groceries because I'm the cook and I worked less. She ran classes full-time from her home office.

The more I talk to my fishing buddies the more I hear that many of them fished hard throughout the pandemic and, as one might expect, overfished. My right shoulder has been screaming bloody murder at me for some time now. I smartened up and stopped fly casting, stowing the rods in the basement so I wouldn't sneak in a trip. I started icing the shoulder, taking ibuprofen, and praying it would disappear. As another opening day loomed near, I feared my inability to swing a fly rod and had to back off.

In the winter of 2021, I had packed away my fly rods. Days later, Mac Lord, my buddy and fly casting mentor (Master Casting Instructor, Fly Fishers International), rang and asked if I'd like to go ice fishing. He and I are a lot alike in our endless energy to chase fish and our time together is peppered with the latest antics.

I said, "Yeah, but I can't dig those darn holes or haul stuff. My shoulder is on fire!"

Mac snorted. "No problem, Suz," he said. "We got this and my shoulder's screwed up too." Seems I'm not the only angler out there overdoing things!

I added, "I gave all my ice gear to Kate ten years ago, so can I use yours for now?"

"Oh, I guess so," came the reply. "I only have fifteen jigging rods." I love Mac. He's a lot like me, or I hope I'm like him one day. He's cool and amazing and a fantastic angler, instructor, and person.

Off we went a week later, meeting onsite, with the sweet surprise that John, another amazing fishy friend, would be joining us. I was in for a real treat with these two characters. The guys were actually minimalists that day and had their sleds loaded with ice augers, scoops, numerous rigged jigging rods, multitudes of jig choices, worms, knives, even a rubber mat for Macy, Mac's black lab. I'm not a dog person, but I fell in love easily, allowing her warm tongue to kiss my cold face. It was heaven. A short jaunt out on the chosen pond to a fishy spot (they seem to know by instinct) and the guys dug a few holes before I was even done kissing Macy. "Let the games begin," I whispered to Macy. She gave me one last warm kiss and we sauntered over to join the guys, both our tails wagging in delight.

According to Mac, John always outfishes him, something I didn't think was possible, but that's what he said and that's what John did. We laughed, barking at each other like old military buddies. "Awwww, Boland's on again, didn't I tell ya?" and on we went through the day. We were hooking crappie (I laughed every time John said "crappie" because he said it with a short "a" rather than the "o" pronunciation of "croppie") and white and yellow perch, until John (of course) hooked into something that

I'm not a dog person, but who could resist Macy?

had his teeny little twenty-four-inch toothpick-of-a-rod bent so much that the tip headed down the hole! A good-sized pickerel eventually emerged. We all cussed the toothy bugger, congratulated John for being the best man on the ice, and returned it to whence it came. I don't even want to catch one of those, but the fight looked fun and those baby jigging rods are a hoot to fight fish on! What the heck, a pull is a pull and winter needs to be broken up by a few.

The local pond we visited seemed packed with crappie and white and yellow perch. My dad wrote an article on ice fishing and I learned some things I didn't know, like that perch school heavily so if you catch one you're bound to catch many more. If you're catching some it may be wise to stay at a productive hole, in hopes of continued success, but they can move so jumping around with a fish-seeking device may be necessary to relocate them. As Dad says, that's fishing!

Dad wrote:

> Considered primarily a lake fish, yellow perch are caught all the way from Eastern Canada to South Carolina. Perch popularity has brought about a lot of stocking earlier years in their discovery. Their numbers and flavorful eating have enhanced their popularity. And, with robust availability in winter ice fishing a great table fish enjoys seasonal popularity. A mess of perch can get a skillet heating for any winter angler missing a fish meal. We skin ours, roll them in cornmeal and flour with a dash of garlic. You're going to need a mess of them but that is the way they travel so you should have a bunch.

I think both white and yellow perch are really tasty but if I had to vote for one it would be whites. On the day I was out with my buddies, we caught some pretty nice white perch with the yellows being quite small.

Mac is a tad on the geeky side, and that's a compliment. He likes electronics and details, so when the situation fits his fishy brain, he can really go to town. As a Master Casting Instructor and one of the most renowned at L.L. Bean as well as around the world, he introduced the use of online coaching apps to videotape students and feed casting tips back to them. Both John and Mac had their fishing sonars on this day, but Mac was my ice-fishing coach and was tailing me with the device, dropping the sonar float in every hole I moved to. It was a riot. He'd say "I got nothing, let's try another," or "incoming . . . hold on, a mess of fish . . . five feet . . . four . . . three . . . two . . . one . . . hit!" and sure enough, I'd have a strike and be onto a fish. At one point he was holding my line off the tip and hand-jigging to hook fish, then I'd set and bring them up. I learned that Macy doesn't only kiss humans. She tries to lick the fish when they emerge from the ice hole! It was wicked fun. I felt eight years old again for a bit there. All this went on while John quietly studied his flasher and outfished us, disregarding our snide comments and accusations of cheating. He's kind of a quiet, contemplative guy. I think he was spitting on his jig, not sure.

We fished into the dark, every ten minutes declaring, "This is the last drop, I'm cold," and, like most anglers, kept fishing like it was never said. The infamous statement "Last cast!" was repeated several times. My coffee thermos had gone dry hours earlier! Our spouses all know, with eyes rolling skyward, an empty thermos usually means last cast—that is, until I say it again or catch another fish. Then all bets are off. We were cold, hungry, tired, and done by five, dusk at this time of year. I'm certain the newest fish stories over dinner were conjuring up visions of more gear and obsession in the house. I was hooked and I could jig with my strong left arm while my tired right shoulder rested. What's the harm really? It keeps me off the streets, out of the bars, and home by dark!

In the days following the fun with Macy and the guys on the ice, all I could think about (in addition to Macy's warm kisses) was gearing up, at least in a minimalist sort of way. I ordered a jigging rod and a variety pack of jigs online, then couldn't resist a second one at L.L. Bean (in case I take a friend not geared up). I found teeny mealworms at a local pet food store, in various-size cups containing one hundred to five hundred. I bought the upper amount because it was only midwinter. I discovered a nearby stocked pond within twenty minutes of the house and, of course, I was there within a week of my first ice-fishing trip. It became an almost daily obsession. With a friend in tow, because ice fishing is always more fun with another, we hit that pond, chipping through three holes with a handy little ice pick I also acquired (not so good on the shoulder). Within thirty minutes we were both getting hits and landing a dozen brookies up to eleven inches in a few hours.

I invited Bri to try her hand on the ice with me. Open water fly fishing had slowed with the cold of winter, but we were both game for the ice and gave it a try. She brought her sweet dog, Nelson, along, and it turns out Nelson likes to lick fish to death also! This was the second dog within a month that I loved having by my side on the ice. He got so excited when we landed fish and was just too adorable sitting on his warm blanket with Bri's spare coat over his shoulders.

Both of us well-prepared for the outdoors, backpacks loaded with gear, essential hot drinks, calories, and the blanket for Nelson to sit on, we set out for the short hike in. Although there is a parking lot right at the pond location we both preferred the exercise. Within ten minutes on site her little jigging rod was doubled over and that familiar smile of being *on* appeared on her face. Nelson immediately put his cold, wet nose in the hole to help land the fish, a ten-inch brookie that broke the dry spell between us.

We each caught a small brookie on this particular cold day, but it was the chatter, chocolate doughnuts, dark roast, and laughs that capped it so nicely. Those fish are back in the icy waters to grow larger. The pond is stocked each fall for winter ice fishing and attracts many families with kids, on days they are not in school. I learned to go during the week and would often have the entire pond to myself, with only the sound of the ice shifting under my feet, or birds being heard.

I think most people who enjoy fishing just have to feel that tug every few days or weeks (depending how strong the obsession), and like good addicts, will go to any lengths to find that hit. Seeing how easy it is to fish a local pond, I went back there a dozen times in one winter, some days freezing my tail off and wishing the cold away. During early 2022, I lifted twenty small fish in two hours, with one up to fourteen inches, a monster for this little place stocked with some six hundred ten-inch brookies. The manager of the place was happy I was returning them to grow bigger for the kids that would soon discover this treasure. I think I've pulled up a sixth of the brookies stocked there and fed a lot of mealworms to those hungry buggers.

My fishing slowed as winter wore on, and locals were catching on to the place, as evidenced by the holes I began to see each visit. Heck, I watched one guy drive up, drill five holes with his power auger, drop his flags in and retreat to his car, never to be seen again! I finally figured out Mr. Outdoorsman was sitting in his car on his phone. Heck, I even saw a few of his flags go vertical, but he didn't. By the time he quit and pulled his gear, his hooks were probably all stripped bare. It was forty-eight degrees out that day! I was sunburned by the time I left. All right, so there was no harm done, but I'm in it for the fresh air, to escape social media, and to actually *feel* the tug in my hands. To each their own. I prefer to be outside in whatever Mother Nature has to throw at me, holding a rod and actively engaged in my fishing.

Chapter Sixteen
Rainy-day People

I come from a family of weather buffs. We watch it like hawks on a daily basis and plan our days outside for and around it. During my thirty years in the Coast Guard I had to know what was incoming, projecting hurricane tracks as they marched through our Gulf coast religiously from June to November. Sandy, my twin sister, and her family live in the New Orleans area and can track hurricanes better than the National Hurricane Center, flagging them as they spawn off of Cape Verde, Africa and watching them all the way to the continental United States. We picked up weather early in our time together so if you ever want to know the forecast, ask a Daignault. I still visit my parents and if they aren't watching something else, the Weather Channel is on in the background of their living room.

Growing up and spending summers on Cape Cod, we were not watching the weather on TV and rarely saw hurricanes, but I think we could smell storms coming. We were connected to civilization and knew when something serious was tracking our way. Fishing was why we were there so we kept tabs on things. Other campers and fishermen on the beach would be abuzz with the word if anything bad was coming. That was our Weather Channel.

Dad's story "Hurricane," in *Twenty Years,* described some epic fishing in lousy weather that could drive most to saddle up and head home. We were on Race Point Beach in Provincetown. Everyone had left the beach proper, but we were hunkered nearby. I believe Dad fell asleep despite the storm. I'll let him tell it:

> I don't know how long I was out, maybe two hours, when a roar, accompanied by a pause in the rain, woke me while the buggy listed on its springs. No doubt what we felt was the ninety mile gust that Chatham radar reported later. The recent advisories had placed the storm center at the mouth of the Connecticut River with winds on the outside well east of the Cape. There was relief that we were being spared the full force of the hurricane, what little we did have passing quickly. By early afternoon the rain had stopped and everybody was anxious to get back out on the beach, wondering if they were going to be credited with a half day for the time spent in the parking lot.
>
> The passage of all this low pressure caused a surge of wind out of the sou'west that I knew would have Race Point in a dither. But everybody was standing around kicking tires, waiting for clearance from the authorities. We fired up the two machines amid a torrent of 'It's guys like you that spoil it for everybody' and went fishing. Somebody had to make certain the beach was safe.

We all fished to exhaustion on that stormy day, hauling literally a ton of fish, according to my father.

My experience fishing as a kid with my family taught me about foul weather fishing. We fished in everything. I don't have the scientific explanation of why fishing seems better in the rain or why low pressure areas that come with foul weather trigger the fish to eat. Here in Maine, when I see a rainy day or big storm approaching, and the tide is right for my area, I'm loaded and ready for what I see as a high-stakes bet on improved fishing. I recall one Sunday morning in late May 2018, not long after the first stripers had migrated north to our latitude, a cool pouring rain was underway outside my bedroom window. It sure sounded better to stay in the sack with the warm fire burning, local news tuned in, and a hot cup of dark roast in my hand … but I knew the cards were stacking in my fishing favor, as uncomfortable as the prospects looked outside.

Forcing myself up, gulping coffee between adding layers, waders, rain jacket, hat, and eight-weight fly rod in hand, I tripped down the forty stairs from our property to the waterline with the perfect incoming half-tide just forming up my favorite homeland rip. I inhaled one last slug and left my mug on the rail, knowing that would only make me have to drop waders and drawers sooner than I wished for a pee I'd need in an hour. There's a feeling many of us know when we're approaching a favorite fishing spot at the perfect time, under the perfect (awful) conditions and we just *freakin' know* we are going to catch fish! It's a vibrating, resonating, *Oh-my-God, I-know-they-are-there-and-I'm-going-to-catch-them* undeniable feeling of impending success. It's cocky and smug and presumptuous as hell and it happens to me when I just have it right. I have been wrong once or twice but I've forgotten about those stories and they aren't worth telling. It was pouring out and I'm cold before the fly is off the rod keeper but gosh, it is fishy.

First cast . . . I was still paying out some loose line from my spool, letting the incoming tide pull it tight, wanting to tighten things up, stripping line through the cuff of my shirt to clean and stretch it, when suddenly it came tight and the fish was hightailing it to the opposite shore of the sound. Of course, my thoughts went to I knew it, darn, I knew it! The line wrapped around one of my fingers, not really being warmed up and ready for action yet, and the fish was gone. I stripped that cast in and made a longer second cast, this time with a clean and stretched line and I settled into a stance of I'm ready now you buggers, bring it on! The fifty-foot cast now barely in the water, rod tip down, stripping, and I was on again. This fish headed to my right, against the tide, something a larger fish usually does, then proceeded to go deeper in twenty feet of water, another typical larger fish antic. My mind raced to this is not schoolie as I tightened down my drag one more turn. Then came the snap, having been left out to dry by a bull that rubbed me off on a bottom boulder saying "see ya" with my favorite clouser. Now I was getting pissed, but I had at least forgotten about the pounding rain.

Third cast is longer, and I pay out more line to get a good drift because the incoming tide is pulling hard now and they often hit as the fly sinks and drifts. My drag is set correctly and everything is snug as a bug. The *second* the line is tightening and fly rising to the surface, I am tackled by another decent fish. I have no running line to take so this fish immediately proceeds to spool my ninety feet of fly line and half of my 250 yards of Dacron (insurance line), heading with the current and across the sound toward boat moorings and anchors that will surely be the end of this hook-up. I decide to get serious, double down on my drag with faith in my leader and knots, and horse the fish toward me. After fifteen minutes of struggle, I land a nice, twenty-eight-inch bass. Now I'm sweating, although I can feel cold rain trickling down my neck and back, having loosened my rain jacket hood. Getting wet is the last thing I am concerned with at this point. My buddy, a local oysterman, is pushing off in his dinghy so I ask him to snap a shot of my fish as I am so often alone when I land a bigger one. We do this quickly and the bass is released with a tail kick goodbye for me. More water in my face.

During the summer of 2020, I made an effort to make good on promises to fish with friends. I invited Nome and Tina to come on by for the afternoon tide, although heavy wind and rain were in the forecast. Tina was headed back home across the country within days and our chances to fish together were numbered. They were all over it and arrived an hour before the time I was really targeting. I always give an earlier time than actual fish time to be sure we're in the water and ready for the right time and tide. With the incoming tide still lower than the "magic hour" we started to have hits and misses, all swinging long rods in the pretty hefty twenty-knot wind. Then right on time as forecast the heavy rain started, which we were dressed and prepared for. Now both of these women are avid fly fishers and don't need any assistance so in unison we all seemed to snug down our rain hoods and lean into the wind as we continued our quest. When the tide hit a nearby downed tree along the waterline, I knew it was time for the "magic hour" and Nome gave me her familiar wink and nod, almost exactly when I hooked up, mumbling out loud to them, "it's that time!" They couldn't hear me, but knew the idea.

In the next two hours we each landed several stripers while the rain and salt made hamburger of our hands and lines cut through the stripping finger like razors. When the tape I had applied came off, I was wiping my bleeding left forefinger in the salt water to keep it clean, each bitter sting reminding me how much I love this sport. My friends seemed miserably happy, if that's possible. It wasn't fabulous fishing, but it was fun and the weather made it a challenge worth meeting. The wind was blowing so hard down the sound, along with the incoming current that the first forty feet of shoreline was muddied like chocolate milk; I would've found it unfishable if you asked me to fish in these conditions, but we were catching a few.

Nasty, a local lobster boat owned by John, a really sweet guy who doesn't resemble anything on earth that is nasty, came motoring into the area we were fishing so we made way and kept casting. I stumbled over in my soaked garb and asked him if he had any fresh lobster and he smiled to see we were interested. Waving Tina over, who was technically a tourist on this trip, I knew she'd be pleased to pick up some reasonably priced "bugs." She bought lobster and crabs from Captain John, giving me a few for Karen and I to enjoy for dinner and everyone was pleased. The pictures she and Nome posted later that night said it all, while I dipped my own *Nasty* lobster in salted butter and lemon savoring the moments shared together and thanking Miss Tina for the treat. A nasty kind of day had turned wonderful with a few fish and some fresh local fare for dinner. We laughed a lot, shared some fishing tips, took pictures, and got really wet, cold, tired, and happy.

I still watch the Weather Channel often. When I hear a storm is on the horizon, I look at the tide chart, maybe the moon phase, winds and rain, and start to think about when I want to be in the water. While some are canceling their outdoor plans, I am moving my work to accommodate the fishing. Foul weather isn't any reason not to go fishing, but I might not take the boat. It's safer and more familiar to do what's in my blood, climb into my waders and rain jacket, batten down the hatches, and step into the surf.

Chapter Seventeen
A Team Effort

It was August 29, 2021. I invited my close friend,
Cindy, to come fishing for stripers. She's a novice at it and is a
blast to fish with because her enthusiasm is simply uninhibited
and contagious. It's funny and just plain therapeutic for both of
us. We laugh and scream like schoolgirls at every tug and, if one of
us does hook up, we hoot and holler like every fish is one for the
record books. Well, ya never really know that it won't be, right?

I have only fished with Cindy a few times and she's a
Floridian, accustomed to warmer temperatures and humidity, so
in the cooler days of late summer and early fall in Maine, it can
be interesting to see what she will show up wearing. She arrived
on time to the second, which is always fifteen minutes before the
time I want anyone here to fish, just to be sure we don't miss the
tide. Her Floridian attire included a winter hat, tights, a shirt,
fleece, raincoat, socks, and shoes. It was about seventy degrees out
with a light breeze. As she asked if I thought she'd dressed warmly
enough, I giggled and mumbled some sarcastic, but loving, grunt
of approval. We hugged Karen goodbye with a last float plan
of time and location, and shoved off within five minutes from
our dock. We packed two life jackets, three spinning rods, a vest

full of needed gear and cell phones charged for emergency calls
and pictures. We are both pretty prepared types, she being a
retired pilot and me a Coastie. The short boat ride to The Point
is only about three minutes at full throttle and I could feel the
excitement in the boat. It felt like we were headed for something
different. Cindy hadn't caught a striper yet that season and it was
August 29! The southern migration would be underway soon,
so I really wanted to see her land a fish. I had rigged two smaller
spinners because of my sore shoulder, but planned to give her a
mid-sized, stiffer outfit, in case she hooked a lunker. Due to her
lack of experience in anything of size, I was concerned she'd never
land a fish over twenty-five inches without a meat stick, but I also
figured it probably wouldn't happen that evening. Sometimes I
am wrong!

We had set the date to fish based on my love of a nearby
point of land that is, like clockwork, always on for just a one-hour
period. The spot has a point of ledge jutting out into a bowl of
water where the tidal plunge of current that comes with the drop
here in Maine is significant at one or two hours down. Water hits
the bowl (so do fish and bait) and pours by this point where a
ledge sets up an eddy and a slower area down deep, that I believe
fish lie in waiting for bait. They may just swim through, but I
think fish linger in the deep section below the ledge because I
always pick one up down there. I use a three or four-inch, single
hook rubber shad with the barb pinched down for quick, safe
releases (of fish or humans), drifting it deep or even bouncing
it off the bottom, walking the line between a good jerky drift
and bottom snags on the weed-covered rocks. I've lost a few
shad down there, but it's worth the decent fish I've experienced.
They're just waiting for me most visits, and I suspect some cows
like this place.

We approached the area slowly, trying not to let the boat
scare anything that might be lurking about. I am an avid "don't

scare the fish with clanking things on the deck or motors running" kind of angler. I think it helps to be quiet but that could
just be the obsessive bonefisher in me. A stiff southwest wind
greeted us, but it was a nice buffer against the strong ebb that was
already pulling us seaward. I decided to drop the anchor so we
wouldn't have to keep repositioning and could both fish while
catching up on the latest life events we had missed in the course
of summer. With Cindy, it really is more about catching *up* than
catching, but we both secretly hope she will hook into something.

Chit-chatting away like a couple of old hens, we began casting. Twenty casts along she set on a hit, but missed the fish. She
exclaimed, "Sue, that was a fish!" I acknowledged and knew more
would be happening; it was early for the magic hour there. That
hour was perfectly timed with sunset, and it would soon be good.

Ten casts later, Cindy hooked and landed a schoolie, maybe
sixteen inches. At least she was no longer skunked for the season,
so we were happily chatting along with no huge expectations
really in mind. I think we both enjoy the processing of simple,
but meaningful, things in our lives, like how certain relationships
are going, family, money, and home renovations. We often
discuss how we feel about things and just the boring parts of daily
life. We've both shared deeply difficult and joyous times as well,
and we offer mutual support to deal with what comes our way.
Underlying all of the discussion is the eternal hope of a tug or
landing a fish, and I always hope it mostly for her. Fishing can be
like a night in the gambling hall, where we all hope to win, but
know deep down that the odds are in favor of the house. Chances
of catching a big fish just are not high unless you fish a lot (I
do), at night (sometimes), and know where and when they are
eating (yup).

We continued, casting and chatting, casting and laughing,
casting and swearing, when suddenly Cindy's rod went over so
fast and hard, she didn't have to bother setting the hook. It's a

good thing because half the time she forgets to do it and it's sheer luck to land those fish. This fish didn't think twice about what she wanted for dinner, grabbed the four-inch shad and high-tailed it for the open Atlantic, screeching down the rip, riding the current, and peeling Cindy's drag like she had a push-button, kid's first rod. She screamed something to the effect of "Oh-my-God, oh Sue, Oh-my-God, this is something *big!*"

I watched her for a moment. The rod was literally out straight. The tip was down low, pointing at the fish, and line peeling away while she reeled against the drag. I bellowed, "That's no freakin' schoolie, my friend!"

We were surrounded by potential hazards that would result in two crying AARP members, so I started coaching. First I said, "Don't reel against the drag," to which she duly replied, "What the heck does that mean?"

Laughing and screeching continued as I then said, "Raise that rod up high and let her run."

"What does that mean?" she replied again. I coaxed her to the stern, closer to where the fish was running far and wide, straight away from us, now some two hundred feet out and riding the outgoing tide to beat us at our own game. Cindy is my size, pretty petite, but I got an arm around her, grabbed the rod with our right hands together, and anchored the rod butt in her belly. I was concerned she might go over the side. Then I grabbed her left hand with my left on the spinning reel handle. "OK, let's do this together. Pump the rod up slowly when she stops running," I said, so we did. Then "Reel, reel, reel!" as we brought the rod down in unison, gaining some line back to the reel. This went on for several evolutions together, but the monster decided to run again, and all progress was erased. Cindy lost her belly anchor on the rod butt and holding the tip up wasn't happening. The fish was too strong and had a full head of steam. Options ran through my brain; I could raise the anchor to chase it, I could take the rod and get the fish in, or I could let her fight it and just see what happens. I elected the latter and continued my coaching, but things were falling apart.

Our fish had tracked to the left and was in open water and current, away from rocky hazards to the right, but it was beginning to swim that way, and ran deep. I have lost several fish in that area. The hazards included shallow water and rocky ledge; smart fish know they can rub you off on the bottom. That's a lesson I have often learned with the biggest ones. I will literally tighten down my drag with strong line and horse a big fish up to keep its nose toward me rather than toward the bottom. I had a thirty-pound mono on Cindy's rod so I knew I could do that if necessary but really didn't want to play rock-paper-scissors with this mammoth. I now feared that was next and it had been twenty minutes in the fight. I didn't want to kill this fish, even if it was over the twenty-eight-inch "keeper" size and the constant pull to the right without really running anymore told me she was tired and just holding on. I guess I mean Cindy *and* the fish!

It was time to do something different, as we were losing the battle and our striper was dying. Cindy asked if it was a shark or a seal or something else. I knew it was a big bass and told her I needed to help get it in before it died. She agreed, and handed me the rod still with plenty of pull coming from our lunker, I then coached Cindy to raise the boat motor, afraid the fish would get tangled in it when we got it alongside. I was pumping and reeling to get the fish in quickly, while Cindy grabbed the net. When the fish came alongside it floated to the top and that was our first view of her full size and beauty. Cindy grabbed the rod and held the tip high while I eased the net under it, head-first, but only half its body fit in my net. I needed two hands and my full strength to get it into the boat.

Our fish measured thirty-eight inches on my tape, which was duly affixed to the forward gunwale. Then a quick set of photos

Cindy and me with our thirty-eight inch bass.

of the two of us. I then held the fish in the water to revive it while Cindy took more pics and some video of a smooth release. I am guessing it would have weighed in at close to thirty pounds; it certainly was sporting a wide girth. We were both slimed across our jackets and pants, having held it up for the pictures, while gear had been kicked out of the way and moved to get around on the deck during the fight. The boat looked like it had been in a storm. We sat and just laughed, not believing what had happened. "Nice fish," I said. She laughed and said she didn't think she had caught it. "Well, we both did. You hooked it, I hauled it." And we roared together with a hard smack of a high five, then kept fishing.

I think we fished another half hour while recounting the events as sort of a fiasco and miracle we landed that fish. We agreed it was a team effort and we were fortunate to catch and release it in healthy shape. We slowly motored home to share the news with Karen, who'd already been texted the best picture of our catch. Like most excited anglers, we did the play-by-play again for Karen, who sweetly appeased us with her shared excitement and listening ears. I think Cindy and I have shared our pictures with dozens on Facebook and over text with friends and loved ones, garnering numerous accolades and compliments. Some of my neighbors were yelling profanities of joy and friendly jealousies the next day at the street corner, while waiting for the school bus. That fish was the biggest striper I landed since my forty-two-inch bass, caught from a kayak many years before, about three miles from where we were fishing that evening.

This fish was really so special because it was hooked by one of my good friends. Yes, she needed help getting it in and I feel like I also caught the fish, but she hooked and fought it in the hardest moments, while a fish is most feisty. The memory will never wear thin.

Chapter Eighteen
Plum Crazy

In August 2021, a friend of mine from my Academy days called a meeting of the women of the Class of 1983 at her place on Plum Island, a barrier island in Newburyport, Massachusetts. Her mother had passed away a year before and left her the house on 49th Street, right along the beach. Annmarie grew up in the place and it's covered with pictures and memories of her family.

Marcia, a dear friend who had been my roommate for much of my four years at the Academy, and I decided to make a day trip to see the gang and take a short walk down memory lane. We had a ball, laughed our heads off, and recalled so many things long forgotten with time. They knew I was an avid angler and wanted me to take fishing gear, but I opted not to. Instead, we floated in the calm, refreshing waters of Plum Island, leaning on noodles and floaties with our hats and sunglasses on. It was pure heartful fun.

While there, Annmarie invited me to come back some time to stay and assured me the house wasn't used much. Her offer was sincere, and I took it at face value, all the while thinking "Hmmmm, this would be a nice getaway and the stripers stick around at least a month longer than Maine before migrating south in November." I know, I know, it is *always* about the fishing. Marcia and I headed home late that August day with our hearts full, having had a genuinely nice time, and my fishy brain began to plant the seeds for my visit back to the island.

Annmarie's house is near the north end of Plum Island, in a cluster of homes on or near the beach south of the Merrimack River. Her house is not on the beach, but is about a hundred-yard walk to the edge of the dunes, an easy jaunt to hit the beach or get to the water.

In the last week of September, I arrived at the beach house around one in the afternoon. It was overcast and very windy. My belongings included bare essentials of food, toiletries, a mid-sized spinning rod, and some lures for spin casting. I knew the forecast was heavy surf and wind most of the week, so I did not bring fly fishing gear. My arrival day was uneventful as I settled in with a beach walk to the Merrimack River breachway, then to a sand bar further south on the island with my spinning rod shouldered and ready. I took a few dozen casts in the five-foot breakers along the beach while walking and saw no signs of fish. Yet I was happy to be walking with the sand in my toes and wind in my hair. I was sixteen again, the week after turning sixty.

On day two, the overcast and windy conditions persisted. Nevertheless, I followed through on my plan to visit the Parker River National Wildlife Refuge. This beautiful place is a vital feeding, resting, and nesting habitat for migratory birds. It includes more than forty-seven thousand acres of sandy beach and dune, cranberry bog, maritime forest, shrub land, and freshwater marsh, but is mostly salt marsh. In addition to its mission of con-servation, the refuge provides a variety of excellent recreational activities including surf fishing, wildlife observation and photog-raphy, and seasonal waterfowl and deer sighting opportunities. It truly is a beautiful and special place.

Karen planned to join me at the house the following day, so as I walked I took note of parking, hiking, and scenic overlook opportunities. Annmarie had told me to go right to the end at Sandy Point to park and walk the beach there for more remote beach access and seashell hunting. I walked for miles and saw a few anglers, including one guy who reported a forty-pound bass landed at sunrise in the area. My fishy brain did a little twirl.

Back at the house I napped, then had a whoopie pie washed down with double dark. I was going to give my first serious shot of fishing to the area near the beach house. It was around three when I stuck my nose out onto the beach and the gale hit me smack in the cheeks. Very few people were out. I wore a shortie wetsuit to keep warm, but allow easy wet-wading, had a rain jacket although it was clear, and was barefoot, because I love the sand in my toes.

What followed was quite unexpected. I looked left, then right, then left again, and right, as I could not believe my eyes. Seagulls and terns were frantically hitting the water in both directions. My brain clicked on, my legs went to full throttle and somehow, I decided to go left first, though no one was on the beach other than a few people walking their dogs. I had the run of the place, quite literally. I had two four-inch, single-hook rubber shad and one popper (topwater plug) in my surf bag. I was rigged with a seven-foot L.L. Bean light surf rod, the four-piece Travel Series only rated for sixteen to twenty pounds because it was easy to pack, and I didn't think I would be fishing much. I was *so* wrong!

The birds kept working, port and starboard, while I made short casts with my shad, and before I could even put my hand on the reel handle, I was on to a fish with each cast. The shad never got to sink, the fish were not even considering the meal choices, but slamming the first thing they saw, whether it was real or not. I couldn't use the popper because fishing the topwater would surely get me hung into a bird, resulting in my having to cut the line, hurt the bird, *and* likely lose my third plug and only popper. It also had two treble hooks on it, something I feared was too much to be trying to remove from the mouths of what appeared to be all small fish. Wrong again!

In the next two hours, I can only say I saw what reminded me of some blitz conditions we hit on the Cape on some days when bass were pressing bait schools against the beach. The bait and stripers were up against the beach so tight that they were in the breakers, rolling in the waves and washing up with the breaking surf. Some hit against my legs as I waded in my wetsuit. I had planned to boogie board, but it became my wading outfit that week. Stripers were coming out of the water, doing cartwheels after the bait. I landed around twenty fish in those two hours before it slowed and my arms became wet noodles. I was tired, tight, and spent. My hands had become hamburger, cut by slipped hooks, gill plates, and dorsal fins. It was my own personal blitz, all afternoon. I snapped a few selfies on the beach with my cell phone, since no one ever came close enough to me to take a picture for me. By five, it was over, and I was done. Cold dinner, a look at my pictures, a call home to share the craziness, and I think I drifted off on the Red Sox losing to someone in the wild card chase, disgusted with the baseball, but ecstatic with the fishing.

Day three was Thursday and I knew the tide was an hour later in the day. I had time to run to my parents' place for a long lunch (it was my sixtieth birthday) and dodge the usual busy traffic hours, making it back in time for what I hoped would be a repeat performance. We ate tuna subs from Subway and Mom had ordered my favorite, the most lovely lemon cake on God's green earth. I waited for Dad to rise from a nap before telling the story of the day before. I knew they were thinking as I was—*get out in time for the tide after lunch!* My parents support everything

I am, and I love them so much for that. By two that afternoon, I was shoving off armed with a can of Starbucks Nitro Sweet Cream cold brew. Mom warned me not to get a speeding ticket in my haste and we laughed together at what we all understood was top priority to go back to Plum Island on time for the tide, but not to get hurt doing it.

I made the two-hour drive in an hour and three-quarters, with little traffic, chasing my electronic map as directly as I could. When I hit the sidewalk to the beach house, I had everything for the fridge in my arms for one trip in, stripped and pulled on my shortie wetsuit on, then grabbed a water for my surf bag and headed for the dunes down the street, rod like a rifle over my shoulder, rigged and ready. It was just after four, an hour after the magic tide the day before. When I crested the dune and came into view of the ocean, there they were again, birds smashing the water and fish boiling after bait! I went left again toward the larger crowd of gulls. Juvenile Atlantic menhaden, or peanut bunker, are like the potato chips of the sea. Hungry fish can't just eat one. Hundreds of them peppered the sand as bass pushed them up with each breaking wave, and I saw twenty and thirty-pounders rolling in the surf after them. It was plum crazy. I had left the four-inch shad on my rod, and it really wasn't a bad imitation of the peanuts. Two other guys were on the beach popping surface plugs, but were working twice as hard as I was as they can be a lot of work to keep on the surface.

What came next was just amazing. On my first cast I let it fly as far as I could, hoping bigger fish would be on the outside of the pack, like linebackers pushing the gang toward me. Before my shad sunk a few feet I was on, and it was hefty. My linebacker headed for the horizon immediately as line peeled off my drag faster than I had seen in years. I checked the drag and, if anything, it was too tight, but my confidence in the thirty-pound test buoyed my effort as I let her run. She took a breather and

I regained about five feet of line to the spool, then off she went again. I was beginning to worry about getting spooled. Being spooled, where the fish strips all the line off the reel until what remains is the tidy little arbor knot that holds (or held) the line to the spool, is a lonely, sinking feeling. I recalled my Dad reminding me as a youth that the drag tightens as the spool gets smaller. The problem is that when getting spooled, you loosen the drag and you are surely doomed. Once that arbor knot is reached, it'll break off on any fish that has already done all that damage. The best thing before *the end* is to tighten things down and fight, and pray, and hope, or whatever you do when things look bad. I did all of the above and she turned toward me as I recouped another twenty feet of line. Then she was tired, so with repeated rod pumping and reeling I could feel my arms shaking as I spoke out loud, to no one listening, "Don't lose this fish . . . Oh-my-God, this is big, don't lose it."

It took me thirty minutes to get the monster to my feet, with the final act being what I learned as a kid, to let the fish surf a wave onto the beach rather than break off trying to beach it against retreating water. I don't know if my fish or I were more tired but there she was, my third greatest personal best. With cut and trembling hands I pulled the measuring tape out of my bag and took a quick measure. Forty inches. I snapped some cell phone selfies and hugged my fish to the waves to release her. My hand didn't fit around her tail—but it did fit easily into her mouth almost to my elbow!

I landed another twenty fish, with one at forty inches, one at thirty, another around twenty-eight, and everything else smaller. Who does that? Two days in a row. I emailed my parents a picture and kept fishing, but I honestly didn't care if I caught another. My second to last four-inch shad was ripped to shreds and I had to put my last one on. I prayed not to break off as Karen arrived near the end of the action and gave me her usual

"Wow, that's amazing" listening ear as I recounted it all in detail. I know she thinks I'm crazy and for a non-addicted, non-angler, she does pretty well with the specifics ad nauseam.

Friday came and Karen and I hit the Wildlife Refuge in the morning, with plans for me to be on the beach by three, since it seemed on the former days I had walked into the party that had started without me. We were there. I was ready. Karen had her book, chair, and camera ready. Birds worked, bait stayed in the water, and bass chased them, but it was nowhere near the frenzy of the days before. I think Karen figures I made all that up. In the course of several hours, socializing with other surfcasters who either planned their Friday afternoon casting or came because they'd heard the news (not from me), we chatted, traded secrets, popped surface lures, and swam our shad. Fish were landed, but nothing was of great size or numbers. It was a five-fish day for me, low in comparison.

I had never been to Plum Island before, although I am from Massachusetts. The place did remind me a bit of Cape Cod, with long stretches of beach, dunes, and sand bars that are safe and dry at low tide and turn into torrents of colliding breakers with the incoming tide. I found bass in the holes behind the bar, in the breakers at my feet and further out at the end of my casts. I caught and lost some big fish. I was a kid again, running on the beach after breaking fish and diving gulls. My hands, feet, and arms hurt for days, reminding me of the adventure and I know my parents are shaking their heads and wondering how I got this way.

I think it's pretty obvious.

Chapter Nineteen
Fish Wishes

As I looked back over my life to write this book, I realized how incredibly fortunate I have been. I was blessed with a fishy family, including a twin sister with whom I share so much (and who bought me a new, bigger net because she was tired of seeing pictures of fish with their butts hanging out of my old one). I have enjoyed a fulfilling career that allowed me time and space for my obsession. I have so many friends. I have a loved one who listens to my stories and travels with me, enjoying my favorite sport right alongside me. And I've caught some amazing fish.

I'm thankful, but not yet done.

I am a moderator with an online Facebook group, United Women on the Fly, and have met many wonderful women who are as crazy for fishing as I am. There are more than five thousand women in the group, and they organize themselves to visit amazing places like Christmas Island and Labrador to go fish together. There is encouragement and support at every turn. I try to be a conduit for Maine female anglers to tie into this group, and to share what I know.

I also help connect the United Women on the Fly to our group of women fly fishers (Maine Women Fly Fishers) here in

Maine. I mentor other female anglers by agreeing to meet them out fishing or simply answering online questions or teaching them to cast. I learn new places through them as well and make new friends regularly.

Besides these groups, I have taught fly fishing for more than twenty years now at L.L. Bean. It is my favorite job of all time because I can share my passion for a sport I love and help others to get out and enjoy it. Teaching requires me to stay abreast of effective casting and fishing techniques and remain open to information I have yet to learn. My coworkers at the company know so much and freely share it with me as we teach together. Students often bring fishing ideas I've not considered. I find that new students are much like sponges, soaking up every word and tip they can find. There is nothing sweeter than later getting pictures of the fish they've landed and stories about the fun they have had.

Some say those who can't *do*, teach. I don't buy that for a second. Those who teach well can translate what they're doing into how to do it in understandable terms that others can comprehend and execute. At L.L. Bean, I am fortunate to teach with some amazing instructors who also happen to be amazing people. They share their passion for fishing with me and I cannot help trying to do the same.

Karen and I hope to continue traveling to beautiful places, and fortunately for me, fish frequently in beautiful environments. We plan to go to Christmas Island, the Seychelles, Patagonia, Labrador, New Zealand, Australia, and more, and you can be sure I will pack for fishing. We also want to return to Turks and Caicos, Belize, Costa Rica, Puerto Rico, and many islands in the Bahamas. So many places, so many fish, so little time. I don't just fish in these awesome places, though, we hike, swim, snorkel, drive around and see the sights, and taste the local fare, while meeting other tourists and locals.

Not to brush past the many wonderful fisheries right here in the United States. I have never visited the western rivers that include a list that could keep any savvy angler tying on new tippet for a year: the Colorado, San Juan, Yellowstone, Bighorn, South Platte, North Platte, Madison, Green, Deschutes Rivers, and on the list goes.

There are various species of trout I don't even know, but are beyond the standard fare of browns, brookies, rainbows, and landlocked salmon we find in Maine. They get big, bad and amazing from what I hear. Many of the awesome women in United Women on the Fly are actually in the western United States and fish these rivers as their home waters.

Huge trout and landlocked salmon of Labrador exist in a dream I just can't stop considering since Kate sent me her picture of a real hog of a salmon she landed on a mouse pattern there. Her story of that monster tackling her mouse keeps me up at

Kate with a huge landlocked salmon.

161

night. She texted me a picture of her fish soon after landing it, leaving me filled with joy for her and hopes of the same one day. I'm guessing she doesn't sleep too well going over that one in her head. We're never the same once we land one of those fantasy fish from our dreams, and we don't get them all. The ones we are fortunate enough to hold remain etched in our minds and give us hope for the future. They fill our hearts and our nets.

My dreams are not just any fish, anywhere. They are more about a few species I have always found to be beautiful in appearance or great fighters. Some involve a "must catch on a flyrod" (tarpon), while others I'd be happy to land in any way possible (peacock bass). Then there are destination fishing locales that any angler would give their right arm to visit and wouldn't consider going without packing rods. Patagonia, New Zealand, and Australia come to mind. You can't get a picture like Kate's landlocked salmon and not truly want to be in her boots. Finally, I'd be crazy not to see any parts of my own country where fish live, so the central and western rivers of the United States will be fished in the coming years.

I have caught twenty-three different species of fish in my life. I didn't even know triggerfish existed until my visit to Anegada, so now I must catch one. Peacock bass have caught my attention with their amazing colors but it's their reputation as voracious feeders (they grow fast and eat readily) that makes me want to catch one on a fly. A tarpon and permit remain the bane of my existence; and although I have caught them on spin and bait tackle, they continue to elude me on the fly. I actually did sort of catch a very small permit while chasing triggers, but it managed to lose the hook as I grabbed the leader and tried to bring it to hand. It was the size of a man's hand—small but technically landed since I touched the leader.

Hunting bonefish in the tropics will likely remain an obsession just because when I do, I am completely and immediately transformed into a brainless, thoughtless creature. My worries fade into nothingness as I completely concentrate on my quarry, first trying to move slowly, see clearly, and get each detail right.

Kingfish, queenfish, barramundi, and various trout of New Zealand and Australia are repeat trips for me that I just wasn't ready for in an angling sense when I first visited there. I fished in Sydney Harbor with a well-paid guide and only caught a bonito; it turned out to be an expensive and disappointing experience, since we never left the immediate harbor. The Aussie island state of Tasmania is a must-do and see for trout fishing. Norway and Iceland's grayling, arctic char, browns, and sea trout all sound wonderful to fish for.

Here in the great state of Maine, I know there are still places I have not seen or fished. The coastal angling remains mostly about stripers from May to October, but I would really like to hit lower New England for false albacore on a fly. I have friends who fish and guide off coastal Massachusetts and would help me to do this.

And who doesn't want to catch steelhead, the "fish of a thousand casts"? For many, the cold temps that often accompany fishing is a deterrent, but not for me. My parents fished for them in their earlier years in Pulaski, New York. A beautifully larger anadromous rainbow trout that has gone to sea to fatten up and returned to fresh water to spawn, steelhead appear to be big and stunningly beautiful. They are one of the hardest fighting fish you can tangle with in fresh water, having gotten turbo charged while fattening up on their salty vacation. Let a rainbow go to the ocean where it becomes a steelhead, and its horsepower boost is appreciable. I hear they can really catch some air—but I wouldn't really know! You can bet I'm gonna find out.

Chapter Twenty

Healing Waters

It was a Saturday morning in early summer when the phone rang. On the other end, I heard a man's voice that I didn't quite recognize. He boomed, "Sue, John Libby here, next Saturday, 0900, Augusta helo landing pad!" I took a deep breath in, thinking, thinking, thinking—and responded the only way someone should when a general tells you to do something.

"Aye, aye, sir!" I boomed back. Breathing, breathing, then asked, "May I inquire into the mission, sir, so I'm best prepared?" I had thirty years in the Coast Guard and retired as a captain, a rank below the general, but I felt like a junior petty officer fetching coffee. The next thing he said gave me all I needed to be ready.

General Libby simply replied "We're going fishing, and wear your civvies."

Again, I replied with a simple, emphatic "Aye, aye, sir!"

"Take care Sue and, ah, don't be late." Click.

Not everyone gets invited by the Adjutant General, State of Maine, to go fishing and I didn't care if we were taking a bunch of three-year-olds out, I was going to be there and be ready. Each state in the United States has a senior military officer, assigned to the role of state Adjutant General, who is the de facto commander of that state's military forces, including the National Guard of that state, state's naval militia, and any state defense forces. This high-level vital position is appointed by the governor and is highly respected among all service members and civilians alike. General Libby and I had met at a friend's Christmas party the year prior, so we were mildly acquainted, and he knew I was an avid angler. His call was both a welcome surprise and a challenge I couldn't resist. Actually, I believe it was an order since it didn't come to me as a question and I do know from thirty years of service that if in doubt, just do it.

I spent the week preparing, knowing I'd be hopping a Black Hawk helicopter, the UH-60. It is a four-blade, twin-engine, medium-lift utility craft manufactured by Sikorsky and something the National Guard uses frequently out of their Augusta airport. That was all I knew other than to wear civilian clothes, not military uniform, and *be ready*. I grabbed a sizable backpack that would be sufficient for a day trip of fishing. I included the following: waders, boots, two rods in cases, two reels, fully loaded vest, glasses, military ball cap, protein bars, water, and a summer change of clothes in case I got wet. I decided to dress conservatively casual in a sporty pair of shorts, sneakers, and a military polo shirt as it was to be a warm day.

I'm one of those on time and under budget types, a bit on the OCD side, but reasonably balanced, or so I like to think. I had just under an hour's drive to the small base in Augusta. I was on base a half hour early, finding parking and the area he told me to be, arriving ready at 0845. He appeared with three minutes to go in full operational dress uniform, which is a working uniform, kind of like the old fatigues and is on the casual side for military attire. His huge hand grabbed my petite one, and I gave him my best respectful shake as he led the way to the helicopter, with the crew standing at attention and the engines warming up. He gestured for me to board first. Promptly climbing in, I tossed my pack to one of the crew as they saluted and jumped aboard like they had done it hundreds of times. I actually have only been on one helicopter in my life in the Coast Guard, two if you count the one I got dunked in for flight training during my first-class cadet training in Pensacola. Now that was fun.

We lifted off only minutes after climbing and clipping in. I sat next to the general as he gave me the mission details during the trip. The Rapid River would be our playground for the day, to join a group of anglers with Project Healing Waters. This organization's mission is "healing those who serve." The Rapid is a six-mile-long river in Northwestern Maine, flowing from Lower Richardson Lake to Umbagog Lake. It is a fine destination for trout fishing and a beautiful location. Project Healing Waters is a five-star organization dedicated to the physical and emotional rehabilitation of disabled military personnel through fly fishing and associated activities, including education and outings. I had been planning to get more involved with Project Healing Waters but just hadn't gotten around to it yet. The general must have read my journal. I'd never been to the Rapid and now I had "orders" to be there. I guess someone had to do it!

He explained we had the entire day. There were a dozen or so military members, but not all needed river buddies, so I would be assigned to someone who needed some assistance. They were already on site and had been there for a day or two, lunch was a cookout mid-day, and fishing was planned for the entire day. I was psyched. Tough duty. All the while, I was ruminating about how to handle a war hero who may have been seriously wounded in battle and needed my help to fish. I wasn't trained in the psychological aspects of supporting someone like this, but I did know how to listen and play the supportive fishing guide so I went with it.

It was a "bluebird day" day with clear blue skies and no clouds in sight. I think the helicopter flew at just over two hundred miles per hour. The ride was glorious, just over the treetops to the river location; it took us over an hour, but I wished it would never end. It quite literally flew by! Light chit-chat with the senior military official in my state, discussing the meaning of fishing and how it could help the men (there were no women in this group). The landing was a simple hover over a small field clearing that felt like threading the needle, but I'm sure was routine for the pilot. Gently he dropped us down, our gear was tossed off as the crew stood by, engines still running, helo sitting flat on the ground like a bird awaiting lunch. Slowly, I began to sense that the Adjutant General wasn't sticking around too long as the bird and its crew remained at the ready.

Only minutes after landing on site, briefing complete, General Libby pointed himself back to the helicopter and began

Me with Alan—fly fisher, Iraq veteran, and hero.

his march back to his crew. All I could think of was: "How am I getting home?" More than an hour in the helicopter getting better acquainted must have loosened my brain and my lips enough to bark out to him "Where do you think you're going, General, sir?"

He chuckled and smiled, "Got a staff meeting, Sue, my driver will get you back later!" and they were off! "Okey dokey, sir," I was thinking. I guess I can worry about that later. Let's fish!

A short briefing was held to go over the plan of the day and I was paired with Alan, a soldier who'd been hit by an improvised explosive device in Iraq and had suffered a traumatic brain injury. He wore a black patch over his bad eye and could see only partially out of his good eye. He knew how to fly fish, was acquainted with the river, and only needed me to help tie flies on his line for him. He was fairly quiet but we quickly became easy companions, only chatting over the conditions of the river, fishing, and flies. I didn't ask a lot of questions and he was more focused on the fishing at hand than his head injury, and that was fine by both of us. I decided to go with the flow.

Alan and I walked shoulder-to-shoulder downriver a half mile because we both could and others couldn't. Some were in wheelchairs or needed assistance in getting around. We fished together for hours. He put me in all the best holes first, insisting I get the first shots because he had already been fishing there. I tied on his flies, as he wished. I knew not to try to educate him as he was more informed than I about the river and the fishing. We talked casually. He told me about his injuries but did not mention how it happened. I didn't ask. I felt the best thing I had to offer was my ears to listen, my eyes to tie on flies, and my support however he needed or wanted. We landed a few small trout each, seemingly content just to be out there sharing the time. It was a gloriously pretty and calm day. He was a fishing gentleman and a fine person, more concerned with ensuring my comfort and success than his own. I don't know his last name, how to reach

At my retirement after thirty years in the Coast Guard. Front row: Carol, me, Karen, and Sandy. Back row: Sandy's husband Aaron, Carol's husband Cliff, and Dickie.

him, or really much of his background, but he was a hero in my book and I was proud to fish next to him.

That trip was one I am quite proud to have been a part of. It showed me just how much some people have given for my freedom. As a Coast Guard officer, I served in the military for thirty years and my mission was to keep America safe in numerous ways, but I was rarely in harm's way to do it. I was mostly in hotels, on bases, and in the field in situations that ensured my safety. I think the closest thing to worrying for my safety was being underway on a Coast Guard cutter in fifty-foot seas when the entire crew, including me, was so sick we could barely stand the watch to keep the ship underway, or when topside icing was so heavy we were concerned for our watertight integrity and vessel stability. I have been flown to hurricane-threatened zones in the United States before a storm hit, and in the days after. I have been dropped by a helicopter in a Stokes litter on a rocky island in the Aleutians of Alaska to meet my ship. I was on a Coast Guard auxiliary flight when a bird flew into our port engine, leaving only the starboard one to get us to our destination, and I have been in pretty scary turbulence on overflights to assess hurricane damage in the Gulf. But no improvised explosive devices. Alan is a hero.

The general's driver drove me home at the end of the day, as promised. It was the best mission I've ever completed with no written orders, no "after-action report," no review of how it went or the way forward. It was just fishing and meeting a few people who served their country and wanted to fish for a little fun. *Semper paratus*, mates, *semper*!

Epilogue

While I truly enjoy fishing alone for the solitude it brings, I am most grateful to the many friends, family, guides, and acquaintances who have shared so many special times with me. Sunrises and sunsets come and go, literally like clockwork. Tides reach their highs and lows twice daily where I live. The moon has its phases, pulling on the ocean and making each day a bit different. Fishing is affected by all of it, so I monitor weather, tides, water levels, and moon phases. During the shoulder seasons, late May and September, I often cannot decide if I should hit the salt or freshwater options that my home waters hold. It's always a tough decision here in Maine. When so torn, I may actually fish both and have been fortunate enough to land trout and stripers on the same day! I am a fortunate and grateful angler who seeks a daily reprieve from life's challenges. Even on good days I want to try. Over time, stories have just kept coming, set in a fishing background and drenched with lessons. Over time I became more aware of my place in this world.

I reach as far back as I can recall, picture my young self alongside Sandy, playing in a sandbox, walking the beach, coming of age with other girls and boys, and fishing all the while. It seems to have been an anchor, something we spent much time doing as we grew. It gave me a sense of play, a work ethic, comradery with my family and friends, and mostly, a sense of being. I see now why that is a form of moving meditation to allow thought and contemplation, without the busy daily distractions of life.

How have I become the woman I am today, with all of her wellbeing, ability, opportunity, and luck? Why is it that I have been bestowed with so much love, gratitude, and gifts of living? Where did the time go, so fleeting and full, yet empty for it is gone, but not forgotten? I had to write my stories to remember them for myself and to remind my loved ones, but also to entice the reader to go *try* if that's what they want, whatever it is they seek. It isn't to show you how great an angler I am, or to espouse knowing so very much. In fact, fishing has taught me how much more there is to see, do, and learn. How much I truly do not know. I want every little story to be fun, passionate, exciting, hopeful, persistent, and at times, yes, heartbreaking. That's life, isn't it? Go to places and see what it offers.

I ask myself if it was the many great fish, or the many amazing places I fished, or the wonderful company I kept, although, often, it was simply myself. I wonder what I did to deserve such richness. Was it given to me, or did I take it—the time I allotted, the money spent to get there, the guides I hired, the people I met, especially the ones who raised me onto their shoulders to help me see? So many awesome people have taught me so many life lessons. Some of them were anglers and the lessons came on the rivers, on the ocean, or even on the ice; standing in the water feeling the compression on my legs, or sharing a hot thermos with a buddy holding a teeny jigging rod. They taught me fly selection, rod choice, river flows, ocean tides, and the patience of a saint needed to entice a permit to my crab imitation. Then they taught me heartbreak, when I lost that fish,

My parents.

or when eight hundred dollars went out of my wallet and I didn't see a fish all day!

Fishing waters often have a lot in common, whether they are bonefish flats, trout streams, or under the ice. They offer us a reprieve from the stresses of everyday life and a vital connection to the great outdoors and provide the thrill of the chase . . . seeking . . . a chance to make lasting memories with family and friends. For many, it's a great escape.

"Patience and tolerance is our creed" has been said to me by a dear non-angling fellow traveler, and although it may seem a trite comparison to life, fishing helps me practice being a better person. I wait. I endure. I try not to get upset when fish don't find me, and I don't cry when I lose the *best* permit hook-up (note that I didn't say *catch*) I have ever had, that never came to hand. I move on, tie on another fly, take the next step, let go, and look for another opportunity.

Finally, fishing teaches me hope. My friends chuckle because I always say, "Every cast, I think I'm going to catch a fish." I truly do. If I carried that level of optimism to other areas of life, I'd be in perfect emotional condition at all times. It takes practice for me to always hold that kind of optimism, but I'm better than I used to be, and I truly think all will be just fine.

All of my fishing waters infuse the thrill of the chase, the agony of loss, and the joy of landing a long sought-after quarry. But is it the fish or our selves that we seek? Does it really matter if we never hooked or landed that fish? It does to me, but in retrospect, with some recovery time, I realize it may not. I confess chasing my addiction to the adrenaline rush that often accompanies a hard strike, along with the ensuing fight to win a hard battle. Time and experience have taught me to love the feel of the beautiful creature leaving my wet hands back to the deep, possibly more than the initial strike or fight.

It is the release I seek. And so I hope . . . that I have found her.

My favorite tools.

Acknowledgments

A sincere and heartfelt thank you to the many people in my life who support me so very much. From sunrise to sunset, moonrise to moonset, one day at a time, you are there for me.

All of the fishy friends depicted in this joyful project deserve special thanks for encouraging me to write our stories as best I could recall them. These dear ones filled in some of the blanks for me when I got carried away exaggerating size and events that actually occurred. Thank you for sharing your time with me, on and off the water.

To Mom, Dad, Dickie, Carol, and Sandy, for bringing me up and growing me into a life that is second to none. My time is full of many fishing days. I can only wish those days included fishing with them each and every time.. I love you all tremendously.

My sincere thanks and appreciation go to the Islandport Press team and, of course, Fran Hodgkins, for her patient guidance and editorial expertise.

Thank you, dear readers, for being interested enough to acquire and read my stories. May they bring you joy, hope, gratitude, and maybe a few laughs. It may not be fishing that fills your net, but whatever it is, let it fill your heart.

Finally, to Karen Croteau, my soulmate, partner, wife, and best friend, who has given me unconditional love and support in all endeavors. Thank you, dear one.

I love you all. Now let's GO FISH!

About the Author

Susan Daignault has been fishing her whole life, from childhood summers spent surfcasting for stripers on Cape Cod to catching halibut from a Coast Guard cutter while stationed in Alaska. She graduated from the U.S. Coast Guard Academy with a degree in marine engineering and served for thirty years. She is now an occupational safety consultant, a Registered Maine Guide, and a Certified Casting Instructor from Fly Fishers International. Her love of fishing has led her to travel around the U.S. and the world, and she now resides in Harpswell, Maine with her spouse, Karen.

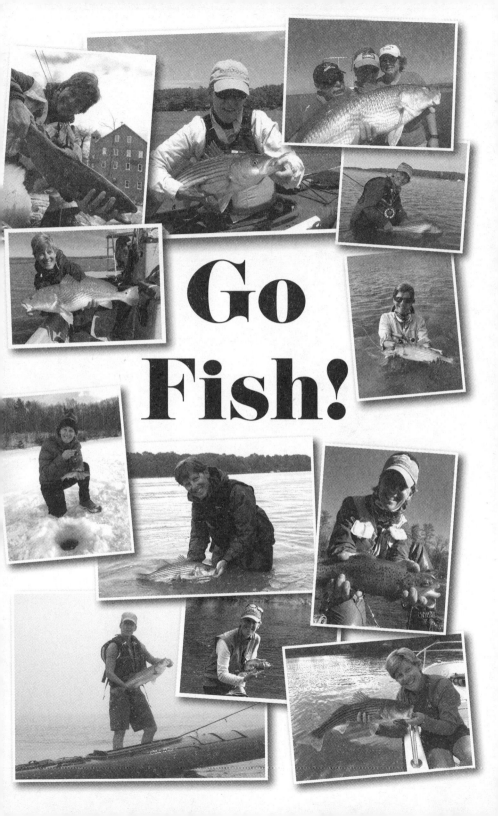

Go Fish!